THE LOUISIANA PURCHASE

MILESTONES
IN
AMERICAN HISTORY

MILESTONES
IN
AMERICAN HISTORY

THE LOUISIANA
PURCHASE

GROWTH OF A NATION

TIM MCNEESE

CHELSEA HOUSE
PUBLISHERS
An imprint of Infobase Publishing

The Louisiana Purchase

Copyright © 2009 by Infobase Publishing

Chelsea House
An imprint of Infobase Publishing
132 West 31st Street
New York NY 10001

Library of Congress Cataloging-in-Publication Data

McNeese, Tim.
  The Louisiana Purchase : growth of a nation / Tim McNeese.
    p. cm. — (Milestones in American history)
  Includes bibliographical references and index.
  ISBN 978-1-60413-052-2 (hardcover)
  1. Louisiana Purchase—Juvenile literature. 2. United States—History—1801–1809—Juvenile literature. 3. Napoleon I, Emperor of the French, 1769–1821—Relations with Americans—Juvenile literature. 4. United States—Territorial expansion—Juvenile literature. I. Title. II. Series.
  E333.M35 2008
  973.4'6—dc22   2008025315

Series design by Erik Lindstrom
Cover design by Ben Peterson

Printed in the United States of America

Bang NMSG 10 9 8 7 6 5 4 3 2 1

This book is printed on acid-free paper.

CONTENTS

Introduction

The city was unimpressive, home to fewer than 400 buildings, including small shanties, where poorer people and working-class folks lived. It was only recently built, the third capital of the new federal republic that had already existed in such important American cities as Philadelphia and New York. It was a backwater in the year 1801. The urban landscape was dominated by the Executive Mansion, home to the country's president; the unfinished Capitol building; and a hotel, a brewery, an abandoned canal, a warehouse, and a riverfront wharf. Outside the town, there was a horse-racing track.

It was almost a completely rural environment, rustic and primitive. Domesticated animals, including cows and hogs, roamed the unpaved streets. Because the town was so close to swamps and bogs, snakes were a constant problem. Wild animals were not uncommon in the American capital, and men occasionally shot at game along its dusty avenues. A bridge constructed across a small stream (its arch had included 13 stones, each representing one of the original states in the Union) had already fallen down. Diplomats who arrived in the American capital, Federal City, today's Washington D.C., from exotic European capitals and royal courts of pomp and circumstance were sometimes dumbfounded with amazement and disbelief at how primitive the young republic's center of government actually was.

Thomas Jefferson, a Virginian who had just taken office as the nation's third president, was only the second chief executive to call the Executive Mansion (which would later be known as the White House) his home. Just down the street, a fellow Virginian occupied a square brick building, where he was assisted by several clerks. He was Secretary of State James Madison, and his job was to serve as the nation's first diplomat. As important as he and his office were, Madison's State Department was so tiny that it shared its small federal building with the only slightly larger Treasury Department. The State Department was the "nerve center" of the nation's international relations. The department received a constant stream of letters, confidential reports, secret documents, and sensitive communications on events that were taking place around the world that might affect the United States. For months, Secretary Madison had been receiving reports of an international agreement that, if true, would be a cause of great concern for him and President Jefferson. The rumors were bouncing from one European capital to the next, all various versions of the same claim: that Spain, the colonial power controlling the extensive North American interior region of Louisiana, had secretly agreed to "retrocede"(give back) that immense territory, one dominated by the vast water system of the Mississippi River Valley, to the French. If true, the rumors were a cause for great alarm in the United States, especially among those intrepid Americans

A farmer works a field outside the front entrance of the White House (known at the time of the Louisiana Purchase as the Executive Mansion). The photo dates from the mid-1800s.

who were moving west of the Appalachian Mountain chain in increasing numbers.

AMERICA MOVES WEST

With the arrival of the nineteenth century, the young United States was just entering its second generation. With that new century, America was changing rapidly and so, also, was the American frontier. The country's first constitution, the Articles of Confederation, had proven to be weak and ineffective. So, Americans scrapped the document, and with it the loose confederation of states, and replaced it with a new constitution. This new framework strengthened the national government dramatically. America gained a presidency, and George Washington served as the country's first chief executive from 1789 until 1797.

During those years, and the four that followed under the second president, John Adams, American population growth almost demanded that the country look west. From 1790 to 1800, the American census rose from 3.9 million people to 5.3 million, and the traditional reasons not to move out to the frontier were disappearing. The Native American population in the trans-Appalachian region (which comprised the lands west of the Appalachian Mountains) numbered around 100,000 people, far too few to effectively challenge the constant stream of migrants headed west. The people living in what had been remote corners of Ohio, Kentucky, and Tennessee began to witness the arrival of more and more neighbors and the development of frontier communities, villages, and towns.

The further west Americans moved, however, the closer they came to the border the United States shared with its European neighbor, Spain. That border was the Mississippi River. It had been designated the western line of the United States under the Treaty of Paris (1783), which brought an end to the American Revolutionary War with the British. Further, as more Americans called the trans-Appalachian West their home, they had come to rely on the Mississippi River for their livelihood. By 1800, the number of pioneers living in the West, between the Appalachians and the Mississippi River, had reached 500,000. Already, two states had been carved out of the backwoods settlements: Kentucky (1792) and Tennessee (1796), making them the fifteenth and sixteenth states, after Vermont (1791), the fourteenth.

Trans-Appalachian pioneer farmers, who produced everything from corn to hemp, wheat to hogs, and cotton to whiskey, needed access to viable markets for their agricultural products. Hauling goods overland by freight wagon was especially costly.

So instead, each year, thousands of western Americans would build flatboats, load them with baskets of corn, bushels of wheat, bales of cotton, jugs of whiskey, or herds of hogs and float their wares down local rivers—the Tennessee, Cumberland, Wabash, and a host of others—to the Ohio River, then continue down that lengthy stream to the Mississippi.

Ultimately, these intrepid pioneer boat captains would reach the port of New Orleans, where they would sell their goods, accumulate much needed cash, then make their way back to their homes in Tennessee, Kentucky, or Ohio on horseback or on foot, traveling overland across a heavily forested trail called the Natchez Trace. Although these western Americans had to travel more than 1,000 miles (1,609 kilometers) to reach New Orleans, the port provided markets for American domestic products. The link between the American West and the port of New Orleans was forged in iron.

The Mississippi River, and thus the port of New Orleans, had not always remained open to the Americans, however. When the great river became the western border of the United States in the 1780s, the Spanish, who gained Louisiana from the French after the French and Indian War of the 1760s, were not happy. They were wary of sharing a border with the United States and feared the citizens of the young republic would move West in great numbers and, ultimately, try to dominate the Mississippi. To make certain this did not happen, the Spanish blocked American access to this vital trade route in the North American interior.

To many Americans, the Spanish move was intolerable. The key to future growth for the United States lay in the lands of the trans-Appalachian West. Congress gave the region much attention; it intended to secure the rights, privileges, and loyalty of the independent-minded pioneers who lived there. When the Spanish closed the river, the Confederation Government of the United States sent its appointed secretary for foreign affairs,

Men load goods onto a riverboat at a Mississippi River landing. The Mississippi River was not always open to the Americans. When the river became the western border of the United States in the 1780s, the Spanish, who gained Louisiana from the French after the French and Indian War, blocked American use of the waterway.

John Jay, to negotiate with the Spanish over the issue, but he had little luck. Security in the western territories for the Americans living there appeared to remain an elusive dream.

In 1795, though, another American diplomat, Thomas Pinckney of South Carolina, began negotiations with the Spanish on behalf of President Washington. By then, the Spanish had claimed portions of the Old Southwest (the modern-day states of Mississippi and Alabama), but a newly weakened Spain had just been defeated by the French in war, which made it impossible for Spain to force their claims in America. Not only was Pinckney able to negotiate a treaty by which the Spanish recognized the 31st parallel as the boundary between the American Southwest and Spanish Florida, but Pinckney's

Treaty (also called the Treaty of San Lorenzo) also reopened the Spanish-controlled Mississippi River to American trade traffic. This fact alone was great news for many of those Americans living in the trans-Appalachian region. The Mississippi River was, once again, open for American business. When time ran out on the treaty, though, the Spanish closed the port again, this time in 1799. The future of American access to New Orleans appeared uncertain.

THE THREAT OF TRANSFER

Now new rumors were flying that Spain had transferred ownership of Louisiana, and with it New Orleans, to the French. Recent years had been difficult between the French and the Americans. From 1798 to 1800, the United States and France had engaged in the Quasi War, an undeclared conflict at sea, pitting vulnerable American merchant ships against the navy of Napoleon Bonaparte, who had just come officially to power in 1799. During this lopsided conflict (the United States at the time had no navy of any size), the French had captured or destroyed $12 million in U.S. merchant vessels and their cargoes. If the rumor of the transfer was true, what might this mean for the future of New Orleans? Intent on discovering the truth, Secretary of State Madison decided to have a talk with the French charge d'affaires in the United States, Louis Andre Pichon.

When the two men met to discuss the rumored "retrocession," the French representative became agitated and defensive. No, the rumor of such a transfer could not be true, he insisted. He knew nothing concerning his country signing any document and gaining Louisiana. Pichon did admit, however, that on several occasions over the past 10 years, since the beginning of the French Revolution, various government officials had talked about the possibility of reclaiming the region that France had once owned but had been forced to surrender in 1763 after losing a war with Great Britain. Surely, Pichon insisted, there was no problem with such talk. How could it be wrong for his country's government to consider regaining territory it had lost only through a decision of war?

Madison was quick to reassure Pichon. No, he told his French counterpart. There would be no crime in such a development. The secretary of state emphasized, however, that such a transfer would be frowned upon by the United States. France was not, at the moment, an enemy of the United States and relations between the two countries were peaceful. As the two men talked, each tried to reassure the other. The French and Americans needed to be friends, they insisted. There was no need to fear any French plans regarding Louisiana. Secretary of State Madison continued to emphasize the message he had been drumming throughout the entire meeting: If France has taken back Louisiana or if she had any plans to do so in the immediate future, such a development might put his country and Pichon's on a collision course toward conflict.

Pichon finally left Madison and returned to his apartment in the American capital. The French diplomat was shaken by the meeting. Immediately, he sat down and began to write a letter to his superior in Paris, the French Foreign Minister Talleyrand. The Americans have heard the rumors, wrote Pichon. They know about Louisiana. If France continues to push for the retrocession of that vast North American landscape and control of the mighty Mississippi, it might result in war with the United States.

As for Madison, he remained uncertain about what Pichon knew or did not know about the transfer of Louisiana to France. Even as the French diplomat denied any knowledge of such a deal between Spain and his country, Pichon had asked if the Americans had any plans to move even further west, beyond the Mississippi River. Even as he sought to calm the secretary of state's concerns, Pichon had reminded Madison that European countries shared the same rivers without any problems. Could not the same be the case between France and

As secretary of state under President Thomas Jefferson, James Madison was instrumental in the negotiations with the French regarding the land that would come to be known as the Louisiana Purchase.

the United States? The meeting had not provided the American diplomat with any assurances. Were the rumors true? If so, what might happen out West? Would the Mississippi River be closed to American trade once again? Could the future advancement of the young republic already lie in the hands of a nation that had been an enemy as recently as France had been? Might there be war?

An
Unsettled Land

At the beginning of the nineteenth century, the hundreds of thousands of square miles that comprised the territory of Louisiana were still a relative unknown to most Americans. Through hundreds of years of European exploration of the North American continent, those lands west of the Mississippi River remained too remote, too distant, too immense for explorers from Spain, England, or France (who were accustomed to the confining borders of small European countries) to get their imaginations around it all. As these Old World newcomers established their colonies of occupation in North America, they chose places that kept them connected to their European origins. All along the East coast of modern-day Canada and the United States, colonial outposts, trading centers, fishing harbors, and provincial capitals hugged the waters of the Atlantic. Some ventured inland along rivers, including the

St. Lawrence, Hudson, James, Potomac, and others, but rarely more than 100 miles (161 kilometers) from the coast. The idea of a "Louisiana" to the far West was almost beyond comprehension, even to the pluckiest of Europeans.

A RIVER FLOWS THROUGH IT

The great territory bounded by the Mississippi River to the East and imposing granite peaks of the Rocky Mountains to the West had been a mystery for thousands of years and would remain so. It had provided the early inhabitants of the seemingly limitless unspoiled prairies of the Great Plains a place to build their homes and hunt the bison that roamed those grasslands by the tens of millions. Those early peoples typically lived along the many rivers that crisscrossed the Plains, which provided a network of natural waterways. In modern-day Colorado, the South Platte River flowed into Nebraska's Platte River, a tributary of the Missouri, which, nearly a thousand miles downstream finally reached the great Mississippi. Water was the key to making one's way across the Great Plains.

The greatest of these western waters was the Mississippi River. Long before the Europeans, American Indians had understood its might, its immensity, and its power. For that reason, the Mississippi River Valley became crowded with tribal settlements and even Indian empires. Along the central region of the Mississippi, near modern-day St. Louis, the empire of Cahokia spread out on both sides of the river, a system of Indian settlements that may have been the collective home to as many as 25,000 Native Americans. When that civilization fell apart, and Cahokia was abandoned, the residents' descendants spread out to the south, along the Lower Mississippi Valley. Some of these people would become the modern tribes of the Choctaw, Kadohadacho, and Natchez. They were the American Indians with whom the Spanish explorer Hernando DeSoto made contact in 1542. DeSoto's "discovery" of these Native

Americans was so remote, however, that almost no one followed him into the region for the next 150 years.

It would be the French, not the Spanish, who would become the Europeans to turn the Mississippi River Valley to their advantage. Their explorers began to see the value of the Mississippi as a great interior highway, not so much for settlement but rather for trade. Their understanding of the river came from their understanding of simple American geography. Having settled to the north in modern-day Canada during the 1600s, the French had established a colonial economy based on trading furs with the Indians. As they reached farther inland to do business with more tribes, the French reached the Great Lakes and the various rivers of the region. Such exploration gave them access to the upper reaches of the Mississippi River. All these natural highways of water gave some French colonial supporters the idea that French colonization might spread from the St. Lawrence River to the mouth of the Mississippi, which flowed into the Gulf of Mexico. Such an immense region controlled by the French crown might one day rival even Spain's vast empire in Mexico, the Caribbean, and Central America.

THE FRENCH REACH THE RIVER

This dream of a great French empire in the New World led French explorer and colonial power player Rene Robert Cavalier, Sieur de La Salle, to launch an expedition down the Mississippi River in 1682. When he received permission in the form of a charter from the French monarch, Louis XIV, to explore only the upper portion of the river and make business associates of only the Indians along the Great Lakes, La Salle ignored the restrictions and headed farther south anyway. (La Salle already held great authority and power in French Canada. He pretty much controlled the fur trade near Lake Ontario.) His party included nearly three dozen Europeans and almost as many Indians, both men and women. When La Salle's explorations proved successful (he made it clear that the Mississippi River flowed into the Gulf of Mexico, thus bisecting much of the North American continent), King Louis XIV forgave him and allowed him to follow up with further explorations. To the French, the Lower Mississippi Valley appeared ripe for the plucking.

King Louis furthered the presence of his nation in the region by signing off on a survey. Once the Lower Mississippi

LA SALLE AND HIS "LOUISIANA"

Rene Robert Cavelier, Sieur de La Salle, was made for the New World. When he first arrived in New France (modern-day Canada), he instantly had visions of a great French empire in North America. Once French explorers "discovered" the northern reaches of the Mississippi River and made claims that the river flowed all the way to the Gulf of Mexico, the aristocratic La Salle longed to explore the river's full length. When the French monarch, Louis XIV, denied him permission to do so, the impatient La Salle defied him and chose to do so anyway, taking along a party of nearly 60 French and Indians.

La Salle's first plan was to build a large ship weighing 40 tons (about 36 metric tons) and to sail down the Mississippi in relative style and security. The original plan was abandoned, however, because such a ship would have been too large and impossible to "portage," or carry, from one river to another. He settled on a small flotilla of canoes, similar to those used in earlier explorations of the Mississippi by French explorers.

Traveling from the region of the Great Lakes, La Salle and his party moved along rivers, bays, and lakes toward the Mississippi. As he traveled, he founded a series of permanent outposts for French trade and for enforcing French authority over these lands.

Valley was charted, towns might follow, each planted strategically to provide support for French expansion. The first such "settlement" was established somewhat accidentally, however. In 1699, an expedition under the leadership of a French Canadian, 27-year-old Pierre Le Moyne, Sieur d'Iberville, arrived in the Lower Mississippi Valley to explore, not to settle. When he and his party fell behind schedule in their explorations of the Gulf Coast, though, Le Moyne decided to establish a permanent

In modern-day Illinois, he founded Fort Crevecoeur, the first European settlement in the area. (He also established Fort Saint Louis, along the Illinois River, on his return trip.) Once he and his party reached the Mississippi, they began their descent to the south, following a wild, meandering river that twisted and turned endlessly. Previous French explorers had only traveled down the Mississippi River to its confluence with the Arkansas River. La Salle did not stop there, however; he was intent on reaching the Gulf of Mexico, to make further land claims in the name of the French crown.

After four months of exploration, in April 1682, La Salle and his followers finally reached the mouth of the Mississippi. There, he claimed the lands in the name of King Louis XIV, stating, "In the name of the most high, mighty, invincible, and victorious Prince Louis the Great . . . I . . . do take possession of this country . . . the seas, harbors, ports, bays, adjacent straits; and all the nations, people, provinces, cities, towns, villages, mines, minerals, fisheries, streams, [and] rivers."[*]

_____

[*]Quoted in Ann McCarthy, The Mississippi River. New York: Crescent Books, 1984, p. 6.

base, because, as he wrote, "the little provisions I had left would not permit us to stay longer on the coast it was necessary to establish a post quickly."[1] The post he established was located near modern-day Biloxi, Mississippi. As for Le Moyne's arrival in the region, it could not have been more timely. He and his men soon encountered a group of English explorers (much like Le Moyne and his party) with intentions to reconnoiter up the Mississippi River. The Frenchmen turned them back at a location remembered even today as "the English Turn."

COLONIZING LOUISIANA

During the years that followed, the French further consolidated their claim and their occupation of the region of the Lower Mississippi River Valley. Le Moyne himself did not remain in the region, but returned to France to enlist would-be colonists. He left his younger brother, Jean-Baptiste Le Moyne, Sieur de Bienville, behind in control of the Gulf outpost. (As for d'Iberville, he became convinced the future of French power lay elsewhere. He died in 1706 of yellow fever in Cuba.) Within a few years, Jean-Baptiste Le Moyne moved his outpost to another location, near present-day Mobile, Alabama.

French colonists of the region proved elusive. There were, after all, few enticements to lure prospective settlers into the Lower Mississippi Valley. The climate was oppressively hot in summer, and Indian attacks were a constant danger. Settlement progressed so slowly that an impatient French government thought colonization to be too much of an economic drain and even turned the responsibilities over to a private company led by a Scotsman named John Law. Some colonists were lured into the region by nothing more than false advertising. One significant shot in the arm came when slaves were introduced to the region. In 1718, a French slaveship, *L'Aurore*, arrived with a cargo of 200 captured Africans, which forever altered the racial mix to include blacks, Indians, and Europeans. Over the following 30 years, nearly 6,000 slaves were delivered to Louisiana, and they were utilized by French plantation owners to raise sugar cane.

The year 1718 would prove important to French colonization for another reason, as well. Jean-Baptist Le Moyne d'Bienville, by then the colony's governor, eventually came to realize that the best location for a French settlement was at the mouth of the Mississippi River. This move led to the establishment of the colonial settlement of New Orleans. Four years later, New Orleans was made the provincial government capital of the extensive Lower Mississippi Valley. During the eighteenth century, the settlement was destined to become the most important port city in North America. The French also established additional outposts. That same year (1722) saw the establishment of a French colonization company that soon delivered "6,000 white colonists and 3,000 Negro slaves to Louisiana."[2] Although French colonists and black slaves comprised the lion's share of colonists for Louisiana, other Europeans were allowed to settle there, as well. These newcomers included hundreds of Germans, many of whom built settlements upriver, where the Arkansas River flows into the Mississippi.

To further develop and guarantee France's claim and occupation of the Mississippi River Valley, the French established a string of defensive forts all along the river at strategic locations. In 1721, Fort de Chartres, near Kaskaskia in modern-day southern Illinois, was established as the capital of the French district of Illinois. Fort Orleans was established in present-day Missouri at the mouth of the Osage River. During the 1730s, French authorities and settlers founded Sainte Genevieve and New Madrid on the Missouri side of the Mississippi River. Such settlements provided the French with bases from which to carry out their trade, especially in furs, with Native Americans. They also established farming communities to produce a variety of grains and other crops to feed themselves and to ship downriver to New Orleans for trade and exportation. In some of these French settlements, including those in Missouri,

AMÉRIQUE DU NORD ÉTATS-UNIS

Bocquin lith. Leloir del. Imp. Lemercier Paris

This lithograph from 1870 shows Native Americans outside a camp offering fur to a trader. Throughout the eighteenth and nineteenth centuries, fur was a thriving business in the central areas of North America.

mining operations were begun, and these produced large quantities of lead.

Although the French frontier communities were scattered out along the Mississippi, they acted as a limited deterrent to British colonists along the Atlantic Coast. These communities slowed the march of British colonists across the Appalachian Mountains in any significant numbers to establish trans-Appalachian colonial outposts of their own. Despite the flow of French colonists along the Mississippi River, and the economic base provided by farming, mining, and the fur trade, the Lower Mississippi "was a strategic outpost rather than a center for migration and trade."[3] By controlling the Lower Mississippi Valley, the French were able to safeguard this region against serious encroachment by its most important colonial rivals—Great Britain and Spain.

Nevertheless, the French did not pour too many of their resources into the region. The overall strategy was to support colonial settlements along the Lower Mississippi, although the French royal treasury did not provide enough investment to allow those settlements to flourish and grow. The result was that French control in the region, so far removed from French Canada to the north, was always a tenuous one. By the mid-1700s, the French settlers along the Lower Mississippi numbered in the thousands at best, whereas the British colonists along the Atlantic Coast had multiplied into the millions.

EUROPEAN CONFLICT

Soon, the British and French came to blows over disputed territory in North America—not the Mississippi River region directly, but another river valley, that of the Ohio. Here lay a region claimed by both European powers, the lands drained by dozens of tributary rivers to the Ohio River that included the modern-day states of western New York and Pennsylvania, Ohio, Indiana, Michigan, and Illinois. In 1754, open warfare between French and British colonials led to a widening conflict that would be known by the British and Americans as the French and Indian War. (When the fighting spread from North America to the European continent directly, it was known in Europe as the Seven Years' War and involved great European land battles and naval engagements in the Mediterranean Sea.)

The war manifested itself in America as backwoods fights in the lakes region of New York and the frontier of western Pennsylvania and Virginia. Such fighting not only involved British colonials and French Canadians, but it also included regular troops brought from Europe to America. North American Indian tribes also took part, allied with either the British or the French. It was during this war that the great American commander of the Revolutionary War, George Washington, saw his first military action. The Spanish also fought as allies to the French against Great Britain.

This lengthy American and European war did not include fighting along the Mississippi River, but the result of the conflict would have a titanic impact on the region. Despite early military successes by the French, in 1759, the British captured the strategic French Canadian city of Quebec and, by the following year, Montreal fell to the British, as well. Soon, the British were in control of Canada. When the war ended officially in 1763 with the Treaty of Paris, the results were cataclysmic for the French. Having lost the war, France agreed to cede control of French Canada to the British. With the loss of Canada, the French saw no way to effectively hold onto their colonial settlements along the Mississippi. Strategically, the French had already ceded the western portion of Louisiana to Spain under the Treaty of Fontainebleau in November 1762. The Treaty of Paris of 1763 required the French to cede the portion of Louisiana to the British, which included the lands east of the Mississippi River.

This astonishing geopolitical development created great ripples of change across North America. The British became the holders of everything from Canada to the Atlantic Coast colonies and west to the Mississippi River, including the previously disputed Ohio country. With the Spanish in control of former French Louisiana, the colonists there soon experienced some serious transitions. The Spanish established their own brand of trade and made political changes, as well. Former French colonists felt so oppressed by the Spanish that, in 1768, a group of French Louisiana plantation owners turned on the first appointed Spanish governor and expelled him. He barely got away with his life, managing to get himself out of the area on a Spanish ship bound for Cuba. The Spanish, in turn, came down on this French-inspired rebellion (at the time, American colonials were engaged in a rebellion against the British). They

This painting depicts the Battle of Lake George, fought on September 8, 1755, in what is now upstate New York. The battle was part of what is known as the French and Indian War, a campaign by the British to expel the French from North America.

sent in Spanish troops from Cuba and stamped out the French uprising. Approximately a dozen French rebels were rounded up and arrested, then shipped down to Havana and thrown into jail. Half were released when they agreed not to return to Louisiana. Five were executed by Spanish firing squads, and the twelfth, Joseph Roy de Villere, a Louisiana planter, died in a Cuban prison.

When Joseph Roy de Villere died, his family demanded to know the cause of his death. When the Spanish refused to provide such information, the family made accusations against them, claiming that Spanish authorities ordered guards to murder their kinsman. As for Villere's widow, she left New Orleans, along with her two children, for the French-controlled

Caribbean island of Santo Domingo (Sainte Domingue). By the 1780s, Joseph Roy de Villere's son, Jacques Philippe, requested permission from the Spanish government to allow him to return to Louisiana. Authorities agreed only after Jacques Philippe swore an oath of allegiance to the Spanish king. Once he arrived back in Louisiana, the son of Joseph Roy immediately filled his father's shoes, taking up life as a French plantation owner. He even held public office, but he did not pursue the rebellious goals of his father.

Jacques Philippe's revolutionary spirit remained just below the surface, however. He never forgave the Spanish for the death of his father, "nor did he stop dreaming of a day when the residents of Louisiana would control their own destinies."[4] Jacques Philippe de Villere could not know that the future for Louisiana would take a significant redirection that he could never have predicted, one he would himself witness. He would one day serve as governor of the Territory of Louisiana, which, by then, would belong to the United States.

American Eyes
Turn West

The uprising of Louisiana planters and their supporters against Spanish control during the 1760s proved a failure, and the Spanish continued to hold the future of the region of the Lower Mississippi in their hands. But all would not prove miserable and chaffing for the non-Spanish residents in the long run. Fortunately, the economy of Louisiana, including that of New Orleans, continued to improve, and planters who had once rebelled against Spanish authority found themselves increasingly wealthy. New colonists arrived, both black and white. Black slavery had never taken deep root under the French, but the Spanish went to great lengths to increase the slave population of Louisiana. It was this increased influx of slaves to the Lower Mississippi Valley that helped whites accept Spanish control. When slave revolts proved an occasional problem for white planters, the Spanish provided troops to protect the slaveholders and keep slave uprisings in check. In time, the white population of Louisiana was dependent on Spanish authority for their own security.

NEW PEOPLE ON THE RIVER

Among those who immigrated into Louisiana during the 1770s and 1780s were Americans. From 1775 through 1783, British colonials engaged in a revolution of their own against the authority of Great Britain, embodied in King George III and Parliament. When the Americans emerged victorious from that conflict, the newly established nation state stretched from the Atlantic Ocean to the Mississippi River, placing them at Louisiana's back door. Spain encouraged Americans to migrate west into Upper Louisiana. The region had been traditionally underpopulated by Europeans. Most were French, who established trading settlements along the Mississippi, including St. Genevieve and St. Louis. For years, both these outposts remained small and even inconsequential. The number of Americans who moved into the region never reached flood stage, but "together with the French-speaking residents of St. Genevieve and St. Louis, they outnumbered those few Spanish officials or settlers who came to Louisiana."[1]

As two relatively distinct populations developed in Upper and Lower Louisiana, Spanish officials began to concede that two ruling styles needed to be used. Lower Louisiana was home to an increasing population of planters, merchants, shippers, and slaves, and New Orleans served as their base. Across Upper Louisiana, traders and fur trappers continued to serve as the backbone of the region's economy. Also, the population of the region was more mixed, diverse, and spread out, resulting in a widely scattered group of people. In the end, the non-Spanish residents (excluding Indians) typically enjoyed a relative amount of freedom under Spanish rule. The

Spanish did not force their customs or language on Louisianians. French influences remained constant, and most whites in Louisiana spoke French. French customs continued in Louisiana long after official French control ended. As a result, Spanish influence spread a mile wide across Louisiana and an inch deep.

Even still, Spain was the official ruling authority, and Louisiana was gaining in wealth. New Orleans was considered for decades as little more than a provincial backwater (one French visitor to the city wrote that New Orleans "deserves rather the name of a great struggling town than of a city").[2] The city specifically, and Louisiana generally, did gain in stature and prosperity throughout the final decades of the eighteenth century. The changes were significant enough to draw the attention of the Americans.

A STRATEGIC WEST

Even before the American Revolution was officially ended and the treaty written that would designate the boundaries of the new United States, influential Americans were noticing and realizing the future importance of Louisiana to their young nation. Some were even certain that Louisiana was vital to the survival of the United States. Two such influential Americans were fellow Virginians Thomas Jefferson and James Madison. Jefferson noted as early as 1781 that "the Mississippi will be one of the principal channels of future commerce."[3]

Madison also saw the strategic importance of the Mississippi River for trade. Americans living on the frontier west of the Appalachians were dependent on shipping their agricultural goods—including everything from wheat to pigs to corn liquor—to New Orleans. Thus, they needed the Mississippi. In a communication to his friend Jefferson, Madison wrote of his greatest fear regarding Spanish control of this river and its increasingly important port. He thought the future of western American commerce was bright; it was one that "nothing can delay . . . but an impolitic & perverse attempt in Spain to shut the mouth of the [Mississippi against] the trade of the [inhabitants]."[4] Madison's understanding of the vulnerability of America inside Spanish-controlled Louisiana was right on target. The Americans could exert no control over the Mississippi River or the port of New Orleans, and both were vital to frontier Americans who had farm products and homemade manufacturers to sell.

Both Jefferson and Madison envisioned the Mississippi as a river that delivered commercial goods, not Americans themselves. As they wrote during the 1780s near the end of the American Revolutionary War, they did not consider Louisiana to be a place for American settlers—just a place for American trade. Today, it seems unfathomable that an American farmer living in eastern Ohio in the 1780s and 1790s, who lived fewer than 100 miles (161 kilometers) from Pittsburgh and a few hundred more miles from such East Coast cities as Philadelphia and Baltimore, could be so dependent on delivering his farm produce to New Orleans, which lay far to the South, a distance of more than 1,500 miles (2,414 kilometers). The simple fact was, overland travel from the western lands of Ohio or Kentucky or Tennessee or even western New York or Pennsylvania was difficult. It was so difficult because of a lack of interior roads, and it was costly by freight wagon. It was cheaper for that same Ohio farmer (and nearly every other western American resident from the Great Lakes to the Tennessee and Cumberland Rivers) to build a flatboat; load it up with bushels of corn, bundles of tobacco, barrels of molasses, or jugs of moonshine; and float it down a local river to the Ohio, then to the Mississippi, then to New Orleans. The facts were simple: Western Americans were almost entirely dependent on the Mississippi River and New Orleans for their economic livelihood.

POLITICAL CHANGES

There was more at stake than just the pocketbooks of hundreds of thousands of American frontiersmen, however. The United States in the 1780s was a new country, one that was unsteady and untried. Its government was tiny, and the reach of authority of that government limited. After all, Americans had just fought a war against a British government they considered harsh, dictatorial, and oppressive. When framing their new government, they created a nation that was more a collection of states whose central government's powers were severely restricted. If Americans living in the western territories could not be guaranteed their livelihood, those same westerners (many of whom were veterans of the Continental Army, which had fought to gain independence from Great Britain) might turn on the government. They might either establish their own new nation separate from the United States or align themselves closely with European powers, such as Spain, that would provide them unfettered access to the markets based in New Orleans.

It was this potential, among others, that led James Madison to consider the framing document of the United States' government—the Articles of Confederation—as too weak and in need of replacement. Madison came to believe that the Articles did not empower the U.S. government with enough authority to either protect American trade interests or even to hold the nation together. By the late 1780s, Madison was leading the charge, along with other influential Americans, to consider revamping the Articles or even scrapping them altogether and replacing them with a constitution that had real teeth. During the long, hot summer of 1787, delegates to a constitutional convention in Philadelphia did just that. The new United States Constitution did provide for a stronger national government.

That same summer, Thomas Jefferson did not attend the Constitutional Convention in Philadelphia. He was not even in the United States at the time but instead was serving as the

Author of the Declaration of Independence, philosopher, and politician, Thomas Jefferson served as the third U.S. president (1801–1809) and the first Republican president. During his presidency, he negotiated the Louisiana Purchase.

U.S. envoy to France. He did support the reframing of the United States and its government, however. He, like Madison, supported a federal system, one that would rest on a strong national government, with the power of the states remaining second to national power. In 1789, when the new Constitution was finally ratified and George Washington was elected as the nation's first chief executive, Jefferson returned to America and took up the reins as the nation's first secretary of state. Through these years, Jefferson was often frustrated with the intense political squabbling of the era, partisan fighting that eventually destroyed the friendship he and then-vice-president Adams had formed years earlier during the American Revolution. By New Year's Eve 1793, Jefferson had had enough of politics; he resigned as secretary of state and returned to his Virginia home, Monticello.

Jefferson did not remain out of touch with politics, though. Within three years, he was back in the arena of national politicking, running against Vice President John Adams for the presidency. Although Jefferson barely lost that election, he was elected as Adams's vice president. (At that time, under the U.S. Constitution, the candidate receiving the second highest number of votes for president became vice president, even though Adams and Jefferson were members of different political parties.) The two had already had a falling out, so the two newly-elected national leaders did not cooperate, and Adams chose to not even confer with Jefferson. Instead, Jefferson turned to his old political friend and fellow Virginian James Madison.

Madison was just leaving his office in the U.S. Congress as Jefferson became vice president. He had been on the national political scene for decades by then, having cut his teeth on the politics of the American Revolution. Madison had been an influential voice during the conflict between the British and their colonial subjects, the Americans. An avid reader and student of history, politics, government, and philosophy, Madison had become an ardent supporter of democracy and constitutional government. During the conflict, he served in the Continental Congress; then, once he managed to guide the U.S. Constitution into existence, he was elected to the first Federal

John Adams was the second president of the United States. At the time of his election, the candidate to win the second-highest number of votes became vice president, so Adams's great friend and political opponent, Thomas Jefferson, was elected to that office.

Congress as a representative of Virginia. Madison also served a crucial role as George Washington was elected the nation's first president:

Madison was everywhere. The president turned to Madison for advice on his inaugural address, and Madison actually wrote the House of Representatives' reply to Washington's address. He then wrote Washington's response to the House's reply as well as to the reply of the Senate. Hardly a raging ego, Madison's actions in 1789 instead reflected his primary objective: to get the government on the right path by articulating the constitutional role of each branch of government. How better to do that job than to craft the first public statement of both the executive and the legislature?[5]

Like his friend Jefferson, however, Madison became dissatisfied with the Washington presidency. This led the two Virginians to form a political party, the Democratic-Republicans. It was their joint answer to John Adams and his followers, who were calling themselves the Federalist Party. Between them, Jefferson and Madison began working to unseat Adams from the presidency during the 1800 election.

When the election was held, its results were awkward. Jefferson had indeed received more votes for president than Adams, but he had received the same number as his vice presidential "running mate," fellow Republican, Aaron Burr, from New York. The election was finally decided by a vote of the House of Representatives. (At that time, the Constitution called for the House to determine tied presidential elections.) Once Jefferson was clearly elected president, he took office in the new capital of Federal City in the District of Columbia, and he soon appointed his friend James Madison as his secretary of state.

Jefferson granted Madison the task of implementing the country's foreign and domestic policies. Between them, the new president and the secretary of state included Louisiana in their foreign policy. After all, Louisiana and especially New Orleans had come to play a crucial role in the economy of the American

(continues on page 34)

NEW ORLEANS: A STRATEGIC MISSISSIPPI PORT

During the late 1600s and early 1700s, the heyday of French domination over significant portions of North America, the vast western region of Louisiana became an important part of their New World Empire. Even though a much larger French population lived far to the east and north, in modern-day Canada, Louisiana gradually became increasingly vital. And just as the city of Quebec was the center of New France and its trading capital, another city served as the great symbol of Louisiana's power—New Orleans. Even though a 3,200-mile (5,150-kilometer) canoe trip separated these two important French cities in the New World, they were for many decades linked as the opposite ends of a huge colonial system that was based on trade and farming.

When it was founded in 1718, New Orleans was placed at "the single most strategic point between the Appalachians and the Rocky Mountains of North America."* The early colonists situated their settlement on the isthmus flanked by the Mississippi River to the west and Lake Pontchartrain to the east. (During the 1700s, the lake was known as the Isle of Orleans). The French followed the lead of earlier Indian occupants of the region who had left a path along Esplanade Ridge that connected with the Bayou St. John and Lake Pontchartrain. Intending to use the settlement as a base for trade, the early French settlers built several small forts along the mouth of the Mississippi River and strung others up and down the Gulf Coast. Despite these outposts, New Orleans remained the most important. It was there that "two navigable waterways from the Gulf to the Upper Mississippi converged."** Along the Esplanade Ridge, the French discovered a natural levee, which would protect the port that would become the backbone of New Orleans's economic vitality.

All this required a keen geographical eye and some serious planning by the French. That planning began at the founding of the site. Jean-Baptiste Le Moyne, Sieur de Bienville, the founder of the French settlement, did not leave the layout of the colony to chance. He set New Orleans off as a great grid measuring eleven blocks wide along the river and six blocks deep. He selected the site of the town's church and its square, then referred to as the Place d'Armes. (Today it is known as Jackson Square.) Where the city's modern-day French Quarter stands today was the site of Vieux Carré, which translates from the French as the *Old Square*.

Although Quebec was built on a high outcropping above the St. Lawrence, which made it formidable in a military struggle and almost impossible to successfully siege, the settlement of New Orleans was altogether different. It had no heights or even great quantities of stone to provide fortifications. The region was thick with lush vegetation, though, which included great patches of hardwoods such as oak, cypress, and hickory. As one historian has noted, "The French built Quebec of stone. They built New Orleans of earth and wood."***

By the 1760s, New Orleans, along with Louisiana, passed out of French hands and into the control of the Spanish monarch, King Carlos III. The city and Louisiana had become even more strategic to the Spanish, who intended to utilize the region "as a barrier to keep Americans away from the silver mines of New Spain [Mexico]."† By then, Americans (then British colonials) were moving across the Appalachian Mountains into modern-day Kentucky and bringing their farm goods down the Ohio River to Spanish New Orleans. Louisiana and the city of New Orleans had suddenly become economically strategic to yet another group of North Americans.

By 1788, New Orleans was still not a heavily populated North American town. More than 5,000 people lived there, protected by the city's wooden walls, with timbers driven vertically into the

(continues)

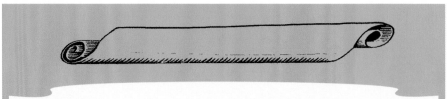

(continued)

ground. The walls rested on great earthworks and included a cannon at each corner. Inside the wooden perimeter, the city featured more than 1,000 houses and other buildings. Unfortunately, that spring a massive fire swept through the city. The fire started when the local army paymaster left candles burning in his private chapel, located in his house. More than 85 percent of the buildings in New Orleans were destroyed.

New Orleans was still too strategic a settlement to die out, however. The city was rebuilt and its port continued to prosper. By the time of the Louisiana Purchase in 1803, New Orleans was the largest and most prosperous port in North America. Even the important American port of New York could only manage to rank number two.

---

*Quoted in Jon Kukla, A Wilderness So Immense: The Louisiana Purchase and the Destiny of America. *New York: Alfred A. Knopf, 2003, p. 31.*
**Ibid.
***Ibid., p. 32.
†Ibid., p. 38.

(continued from page 31)

West between the Mississippi River and the Appalachians. Western trade "depended on the ability to send goods down the Mississippi, which functioned as a gateway to broader trading opportunities on both sides of the Atlantic."[6] That America was moving west went without saying. The tide had been steady during the last half of the 1700s, as the number of Americans more than quadrupled from 1.2 million to 5 million. During the last decade of the eighteenth century, the non-Indian populations of Kentucky and Tennessee increased by 300 percent, and both became the fifteenth and sixteenth states before the end of the decade. (Vermont was the fourteenth state.) By 1800, Kentucky alone was home to more Anglo-Americans than 5 of the original 13 colonies (New Hampshire, Rhode Island, New Jersey, Delaware, and Georgia). That same year, the territory of Ohio was experiencing such rapid growth that it would soon become the nation's seventeenth state.

A POSSIBLE CESSION

To many Americans, the thought of the Spanish closing the Mississippi and the port of New Orleans to American trade seemed highly unlikely. The trade was good for both the Americans and the Spanish, after all. In addition, in 1795, one of President Washington's negotiators, Thomas Pinckney, had managed to hammer out a treaty with the Spanish guaranteeing Americans' continued use of the river and of the "right of deposit" in New Orleans, a privilege that allowed American goods to be stored in New Orleans' warehouses until shipment out to other foreign ports.

No sooner had Jefferson taken office and Madison been appointed secretary of state, however, than events turned against hope, raising concerns in Federal City and across the country like a firebell in the night. Jefferson and Madison received word that the Spanish had ceded Louisiana back to the French. The two European powers had negotiated an agreement—the Treaty of San Ildefonso—that called for France to take ownership of Louisiana, even though the Spanish would continue to govern the vast and strategic North American region. By 1801, many Americans had come to despise and distrust the French.

From 1798 to 1800, during the last two years of President Adams's single term as president, the two countries engaged in a de facto naval war, brought on by French privateering, which resulted in the seizure of many American merchant ships and their cargoes. That conflict was technically still taking place as Jefferson took the reins of national power in 1801.

There was another reason for not trusting the French, even if it had been done so secretly that almost no Americans even knew it had happened. Bonaparte had pulled a fast one on the Americans just the previous year. To give the appearance of being "pro-American," French diplomats had negotiated with a trio of American ministers and signed an agreement called the Treaty of Mortefontaine. It was named after the country manor house of Joseph Bonaparte, Bonaparte's older brother, where the document was signed on September 30, 1800. The treaty appeared to represent a change of heart on behalf of the French, who had been harassing and capturing American merchant ships for years. Under this new agreement, Bonaparte was promising to bring an end to such seafaring abuses. But this highly pro-American bit of diplomacy was followed the very next day (October 1) with a highly anti-American agreement, the Treaty of San Ildefonso, by which the Spanish handed Louisiana back to the French. Bonaparte, it seemed to Jefferson and other American leaders, was playing both sides for fools.

The possibility of French control over Louisiana immediately raised great concerns across the new republic. Perhaps no one summed up the potential better than Rufus King, the American minister to Great Britain, who soon wrote as a warning that the cession "may actually produce effects injurious to the Union and consequent happiness of the people of the United States."[7] Soon, King's words would prove prophetic.

A New American Diplomat

As the new century opened, a handful of influential men, both in America and in Europe, had already begun to determinine the future of Louisiana. Simultaneous events on both continents were unfolding that would forever change the destiny of the vast Mississippi River region that was at that time controlled by the French. Perhaps the initial event that began the ball rolling in deciding the fate of Louisiana was a revolution—not the American Revolutionary War of the 1770s and early 1780s, but a European revolution in France against the royal authority of King Louis XVI. The French Revolution lasted for a decade, stretching along a twisted and sometimes bloody path from 1789 until 1799. This great conflict eventually brought down the monarchy, which was temporarily replaced by an equally all-powerful civilian government.

NEW LEADERSHIP

After a few short years, the leadership in France had become so unpopular that the country was ripe for another uprising. This time, the military would lead the charge to topple the French government (the country was being run by an inefficient and corrupt five-man committee called the Directory). The military coup was led by a general from the Mediterranean island of Corsica (off the coast of France). He began his rise to power fighting various European countries at war with the leaders of the French Revolution. In time, he would turn against the revolution when it failed to bring about legitimate and meaningful change for France. The general who was ready to lead France in 1799 was Napoleon Bonaparte. He would become a key player in determining the future of Louisiana.

By 1801, the year of the closing of the port of New Orleans, Bonaparte was on the brink of controlling much of Europe. Through nine long years of war, he had driven the British into near bankruptcy. The previous year, Bonaparte had defeated the main ally of the British, the Austrians, in the Battle of Marengo. Following that victory, the French general forced Vienna to sign a treaty requiring the Austrians to surrender the Grand Duchy of Tuscany. As victories came to Bonaparte like clock work, he established a great empire over much of Europe. While working as France's First Consul, Napolean was also eyeing the possibilities of another empire for himself—only, this one was in North America.

Another French authority would also play an important role concerning Louisiana. He, too, came to power during the French Revolution. Fifteen years Bonaparte's elder, Charles Maurice de Talleyrand-Périgord (commonly called Talleyrand) entered the world stage during a turbulent period of European history. He would become "one of the most corrupt and devious politicians in the history of France or any other nation."[1] Like Bonaparte, he was born into a minor aristocratic family from Paris "that traced their pedigree to the year 1000."[2] As a young

LE PRINCE DE TALLEYRAND.

This painting depicts Charles Maurice de Talleyrand-Perigord, Prince of Benevent, French politician, and minister of foreign affairs under Napoleon Bonaparte and Louis XVIII.

man, he attended school, received an adequate education, and was appointed by the Roman Catholic Church in France as the bishop of Autun, in 1788. (His father virtually forced the priesthood on his son because he thought him handicapped physically; as a younger man, Talleyrand had experienced an injury that left him with a serious limp.) The role of bishop did not suit him. (Talleyrand was already toying with atheism as his personal philosophy of life.)

When Talleyrand supported the French Revolution in 1789, the pope ordered him excommunicated and stripped of his vestments. In a short time, he threw off his church office and joined the French diplomatic corp. His early assignments included the young United States and Great Britain. As a supporter of the French Revolution, Talleyrand eventually returned to France and served the Directory as France's foreign minister from 1797 to 1799, the year Bonaparte came to power.

When Talleyrand took the office of foreign minister, he is alleged to have said: "I am going to make an immense fortune."[3] To prove himself right, Talleyrand soon demanded a large bribe from American diplomats as a down payment to open up diplomatic dialogue regarding tensions between the Adams administration and the French government. The Americans balked dramatically, with one minister allegedly responding, "No, not a sixpence!" In short order, the response was retold as "Millions for defence, but not one cent for tribute!"[4] Talleyrand's demands soon led President Adams and the fledging U.S. Navy into an undeclared naval war with France.

During those final years of the Revolution, just prior to Bonaparte's coming to power, Talleyrand began to make plans to regain French dominance over North America—power that had been lost following the Seven Years' War (the French and Indian War) in the 1760s. He considered control of Louisiana vital, not as a first step to replanting the French flag again in the New World, but as a means of limiting the power of the new United States. Having spent a couple of years in the United States during the mid-1790s, at the twilight period of the French Revolution known as the "Reign of Terror," Talleyrand had come to know Americans closely and was not impressed. He considered them "boring, self-righteous upstarts who needed to be put in their place."[5] How much better to defang the new republic than

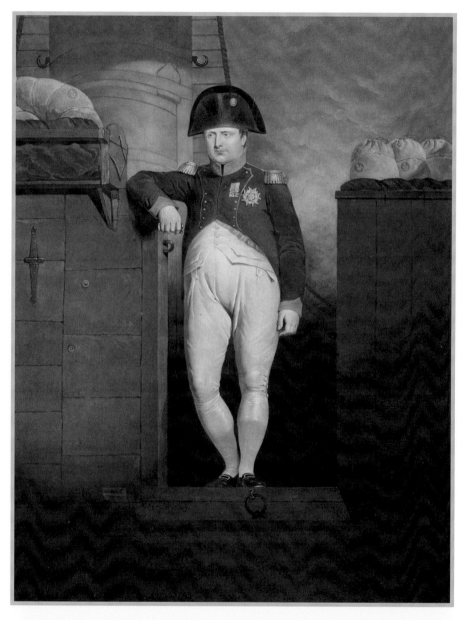

Napoleon Bonaparte was ruler of France during the end of the eighteenth century and the beginning of the nineteenth. Although Napoleon had a secret plan to build an empire in North America, troubles elsewhere in his empire convinced him to sell the Louisiana Territory quickly and cheaply to the United States.

to stand in the way of their ever-westward advance? He set his sights on taking control of Florida (at that time the British-owned southern border of the United States) and the great Mississippi River Valley. Talleyrand intended to erect "a wall of brass" that would stop the Americans in their tracks.[6]

Talleyrand's efforts to wrest control of Louisiana from Spain came to nothing, however. It was not as though the Spanish were not interested in such a deal. As early as 1796, the Spanish prime minister, Manuel de Godoy, even offered to sell Louisiana to the French, but the French balked; they considered the asking price to be too high. Once Bonaparte took control of the French government in 1800, though, his military took control of Spain. Holding the reins of power over his neighbor south of the Pyrennes, Bonaparte held the future of Louisiana in his hands. To make certain that his control of the region would have no challengers, Bonaparte redefined "Louisiana" to include not just the vast territory lining the western banks of the Mississippi River, but also the western portion of Florida, which bordered the river's lower eastern banks.

Systematically, Napoleon Bonaparte had gained control of Louisiana. In late July 1800, he sent instructions to the French ambassador to Spain, Charles-Jean-Marie Alquier, to call for negotiations between the two European powers regarding Louisiana. The following month, Bonaparte dispatched a special negotiator, General Louis Alexandre Berthier, to Spain to work alongside Alquier. By the following month, the bargaining was over, and the Second Treaty of San Ildefonso was assembled. The French would, indeed, receive Louisiana from the Spanish, along with six Spanish warships. In exchange, Bonaparte agreed to establish a kingdom in north-central Italy for the Spanish queen's brother, Ferdinand, duke of Parma. By October 1, the French and Spanish finalized their secret negotiations.

With the French straddling the Atlantic Ocean, France's First Consul had managed a coup. He did so even as he kept his negotiations secret from the Americans until it was simply too late.

AN AMERICAN DIPLOMAT

Few took the news of the transfer or "retrocession" of Louisiana from the Spanish to the French harder than a New Yorker named Robert Livingston. He had been aware of rumors of the possible transfer of the Spanish-held region to the French for quite some time prior to it actually happening. He had even been dispatched to Paris to make certain such a thing did *not* happen.

Livingston had long been in the service of his country, even before it officially became the United States. Robert's great-grandfather, who was also named Robert, had reached America in 1672 from Scotland. Livingston worked hard in fur trading from the New York colony's capital, Albany. He received aid from friendly politicians and was fortunate to marry into the long-standing power family of old Dutch New York, the Van Rensselaers. He eventually became the "Lord of the Manor" of 160,000 acres of land. Following the elder Robert's death in 1728, his son, yet another Robert, built a great estate and manor house on the Hudson at Clermont. It was there that the future diplomat's father, Robert Robert Livingston, was born. His son, also named Robert Robert, was born in New York City in 1746. This great-grandson remained a resident of the city but loved to spend time at the family estate at Clermont, where he was "very fond of country life, of shooting, and taking solitary walks with his gun."[7] By 1801, when Robert Livingston became the American minister to France, his land holdings were even larger than that of earlier Livingstons, spanning both banks of the Hudson River. In New York, his family held not only vast land holdings, but significant political power.

By 1770, Livingston was a successful New York lawyer who shared a practice with John Jay, who would one day become one of the American republic's first diplomats and its first chief justice of the Supreme Court. When the American Revolutionary War opened in 1775, Livingston supported the conflict against Great Britain. (At his graduation from King's College, known today as Columbia University, Livingston had delivered a commencement address titled "In Praise of Liberty.") He was selected as a New York delegate to the Continental Congress and was a signer of the Declaration of Independence. By 1781, with an appointment as foreign secretary of Congress,

NAPOLEON BONAPARTE
1769–1821

France's First Consul

Almost no French leader in history left a legacy as significant as that of Napoleon Bonaparte, the man who tried to right his country after 10 years of bloody revolution. In time, he would become one of the most forceful yet beloved rulers of France. This powerful French figure, who would one day declare himself emperor and conqueror of nearly all of early nineteenth-century Europe, sprang from humble roots.

Bonaparte was born in 1769 into a minor aristocratic family of Corsica that had no money and no real importance at the time of his birth. (France had purchased the island from the Italian city-state of Genoa two years earlier.) He attended French military schools, where he excelled in the study of mathematics and the science of artillery. When the French Revolution began (Napoleon was only 20 years old), he was able to make a reputation for himself by fighting against such European powers as Austria and other German states, as well as Great Britain. He fought and won battles from Italy to Egypt, leading his forces with great skill and absolute

Livingston was placed in charge of the diplomacy of the young nation still at war with Britain. The efficient Livingston quickly set out to establish a foreign affairs department up to the challenge of facing British diplomats while cooperating with their French counterparts. (The French entered the American Revolutionary War as an ally in 1778.) He advised American negotiators at the end of the war to cooperate with the French and, even then, pushed for the new United States to include territory across the trans-Appalachian region to the Mississippi River.

ruthlessness. By the time he was 25 years old, Bonaparte had advanced to the rank of brigadier general. Seven years later, in 1799, he delivered a coup d'etat that resulted in his appointment as First Consul—a new type of leader of France—after the manner of the ancient Romans.

Despite the existence of a new French constitution, a by-product of the French Revolution, Bonaparte soon gained the full power of a strong executive. The country's assembly rubber stamped nearly every one of his decisions, and power surrounded him. As the American ambassador to France, Robert Livingston, noted of Bonaparte in a letter written to James Madison in 1802: "There never was a government in which less could be done by negotiation than here. There are no people, no legislature, no counselors. One man is everything. He seldom asks advice, and never hears it unasked. His ministers are mere clerks; and his legislature and counsellors parade officers."[*]

*Quoted in Junius P. Rodriguez, ed. The Louisiana Purchase: A Historical and Geographical Encyclopedia. Santa Barbara, Calif.: ABC-CLIO, 2002, p. 327.

Robert Livingston (1746–1813) was the U.S. Minister to France from 1801 to 1804, and was instrumental in negotiating the purchase of Louisiana from the French.

In 1783, with the war over and the Treaty of Paris (which did extend the western American border to the great western river) signed, Livingston resigned his post.

During the 1790s, as congressmen and their various supporters began to fall into one of the two political camps (the Federalists and the Democratic-Republicans), Livingston remained involved in politics and gave his constant support to the Republicans. When Jefferson ran for president in 1800, Livingston supported him. In return, Jefferson dispatched his political friend to Paris. Livingston, after all, had already served as a diplomat to France. The American minister considered France a friend of the United States. He was well aware of the contribution the French had made in supporting his country as an ally during the American Revolution.

AN AMERICAN IN PARIS

Both President Jefferson and Secretary of State Madison felt Livingston to be just the man for the immediate task of dealing with the French. Jefferson thought Livingston so intelligent he once described him as a man with a mind of "the first order."[8] He knew how the French thought and was relatively versed in the nature of negotiating with Europeans, and the Americans would need the best negotiator at their disposal to accomplish the mission they had in store for Livingston. For starters, he was to seek damages from the French on behalf of American shippers for losses they had sustained from French privateers during the previous two years of the undeclared naval conflict, typically referred to by modern historians as the "Quasi-War."

Even as Livingston was sent packing to Paris, his hands were relatively tied. Beyond his immediate instructions of negotiating for shipping compensations, he was to determine the truth or falsehood regarding France's intent concerning Louisiana. Were the French intending to take control of Louisiana? The rumors had been constant from the day Jefferson was inaugurated in Federal City in March. That month, American diplomats began sending dispatches "of the intended retrocession of Louisiana to Secretary of State James Madison."[9]

Although such rumors greeted the incoming Jefferson administration, there was nothing new about them. Some even dated as early as 1793, during the earlier days of the French

Revolution. With each passing year of the revolution, and especially as Napoleon Bonaparte declared new victories on the battlefield during the 1790s, the possibility of such a transfer from Spain to France seemed more plausible, as well as more likely. Diplomats from Madrid to London spoke quietly behind closed doors to American ministers, further spreading the rumor of the return of Louisiana to the French. It had become a tale that would not die.

If Livingston, indeed, discovered the rumor to be true, Livingston was instructed to "do everything in his power to dissuade Bonaparte from the transfer."[10] But even with those marching orders, Livingston was also told to be delicate. Jefferson, a Francophile and great emotional supporter of most things French, still hoped the alliance of earlier days—an alliance that had begun more than 20 years before—might still count for something at the opening of the new century. Livingston was "to do nothing that would unnecessarily irritate our future neighbors, or check the liberality which they may be disposed to exercise in relation to the trade and navigation through the mouth of the Mississippi."[11]

These dual orders to Livingston would have strained the talents of even the best of diplomats. He was expected to talk Napoleon Bonaparte out of any transfer of Louisiana from Spain to France, but needed to do so without ruffling the feathers of the French First Consul or even his diplomat, Talleyrand, enough to cause the French to cut off American trade access to New Orleans, should the transfer occur.

Despite the challenges of the Livingston mission, the powerful New Yorker packed his bags and left for France on October 15, 1801, onboard the sleek, naval frigate, *USS Boston*. The "Lord of the Manor" did not travel alone, but took along an entourage that included his wife, Mary Stevens Livingston, "a polite, sensible, well-bred woman."[12] The Livingstons were accompanied by their two daughters, 20-year-old Elizabeth Stevens Livingston and 18-year-old Margaret Maria Livingston.

The Livingston daughters brought along their husbands, both of whom were distant cousins of their father. Also in tow was Livingston's secretary, Thomas Sumter. It was Sumter's responsibility to carry the diplomat's official papers and credentials authorizing him to speak on behalf of the United States. As for the specific instructions Livingston received from President Jefferson and Secretary of State Madison, they were not included in this stack of documents. For security and secrecy's sake, Livingston committed those to memory.

Traveling in style, the six Livingstons brought onboard a small army of servants to see to the family's personal needs, which included carrying "a mountain of trunks and suitcases" along with a variety of the family's livestock, including "poultry, hogs, sheep, and a cow and a calf."[13] To help make the sailing trip as comfortable as possible for his wife and daughters, Livingston brought along the family carriage, which was lashed to the quarterdeck of the ship to provide them with a floating parlor of sorts.

A DANGEROUS WORLD OF DIPLOMATS

The voyage went well, but ended with a harrowing turn. When the ship approached the French coast, a harsh wind blew, as "waves towered above the quarterdeck."[14] The wind made a sudden shift, though, and the vessel limped into the port of L'Orient. Waiting to greet them was the Marquis de Lafayette, who had served as an volunteer aide to General Washington during much of the American Revolution. During the war, Lafayette had been a frequent guest of Robert Livingston at his Clermont estate on the Hudson. Lafayette had experienced great difficulties during the previous decade because of French politics. An original supporter of the Enlightened ideals of the French Revolution, he had rejected its excesses, and had even fled to Austria during the Reign of Terror. There, he was arrested and spent most of a decade in prison for his alleged role in the revolution. Through the efforts of several influential American supporters, Lafayette had gained his freedom. He had returned to France under invitation from Bonaparte, who hoped the old aristocrat would give him his support.

Accompanying the aristocratic Lafayette was François Barbé-Marbois, who had served as the secretary to the French delegation to the United States during the American Revolution (while there, he married an American woman), and was then serving as Bonaparte's minister of finance. He, too, had close associations with Livingston, having worked alongside him to keep international relations between the United States and France on friendly terms. He, too, had landed on the wrong side of the French Revolution. In 1797, revolutionaries had captured him and banished him to the South American colony of French Guyana. During those dreadful years, Barbé-Marois's wife had collapsed mentally and never recovered. As with Lafayette, Bonaparte had brought him back to France, and even appointed him finance minister.

Robert Livingston, his family, and servants, disembarked the *USS Boston* and within days reached the French capital on December 3. Between Lafayette and Barbé-Marbois, the way for the American diplomat was opened. Within two days of arriving in Paris, Livingston was introduced to Foreign Minister Talleyrand and, within 24 hours, he stood before Napoleon Bonaparte himself, with Livingston showing his respects by bowing to the French leader. Livingston's two sons-in-law accompanied the diplomat, dressed in the uniforms worn by aide-de-camps to the governor of New York. The scene at the Hall of Ministers was pure Bonaparte:

> After waiting for an hour, they were ushered to the Audience Room between parallel lines of magnificently uniformed consular guards. There the first consul, in a gorgeous red coat embroidered with gold, paced around a waiting circle of

diplomats, exchanging a few words with each, while Foreign Secretary Talleyrand limped after him.[15]

As Bonaparte and one of the wealthiest men in America stood and faced one another, with Livingston, at 6 feet (1.8 meters) in height, nearly towering over his shorter counterpart, the French leader asked him a direct question, whether he had ever visited France before. When Livingston responded he had not, Bonaparte bluntly informed and, perhaps, warned him at the same time with the words: "You have come to a very corrupt world." Then, the French leader turned to Talleyrand and spoke in a nearly mocking tone: "Explain to him that the old world is very corrupt. You know something about that, don't you?"[16]

Whether Talleyrand responded to the taunt is not known. The taunt may actually have been intended for Livingston himself, though, whom Bonaparte may have quickly summed up as naïve, a babe in the woods of hard-edged French diplomacy. Already, the French First Consul and his foreign minister were mocking Livingston. However, the newly arrived diplomat from New York did not play his hand; did not reveal whether the words spoken offended him or not. It was becoming clear to him that Louisiana was, indeed, in the hands of the French, and he immediately shifted his mission and redirected his efforts. He must find out what Bonaparte's plans were for the lands west of his young country, the vast region that extended along the valley of the Mississippi.

A Lost Cause

When Napoleon Bonaparte forced the retrocession of Louisiana by the Spanish into his ever-expanding empire, his actions set in motion a series of events that would soon involve more geography in the Western Hemisphere than the lands bordering the Mississippi River. One of the other key pieces to the French first consul's dream of a second New World empire lay in a small island in the Caribbean the Spanish had first established as the colony of Hispaniola. Today the island comprises two nations: Haiti, the western half, and the Dominican Republic, the eastern half. The western portion of the island, known then as Santo Domingo, had been returned to France by Spain more than a century earlier, in 1697.

ISLAND UPRISING

Even as French fur trappers and traders were settling New France (modern-day Canada) far to the north during the same period, Santo Domingo's "productivity had made it a crown jewel among France's colonial possessions."[1] When Bonaparte began to flesh out his dream of an American empire, he, too, saw Santo Domingo as valuable. It would provide the jumping off place, a springboard for the thousands of French troops he intended to dispatch to Louisiana. Little did Bonaparte know that Santo Domingo would, in a few short years, work against him, not only failing to aid his New World imperial plans, but instead helping to bring about the destruction of his European empire.

As Bonaparte made his plans to send troops to the Caribbean island, Santo Domingo was already in the midst of upheaval. Beginning in 1788, on the eve of the French Revolution, the island's French population was split between the "great whites" and the "little whites," with each taking sides against one another. The "great whites" made up the group of significant landowners. Santo Domingo's population included approximately 40,000 white colonists, 30,000 free blacks and mulattos, people of mixed race, and a half million slaves. Among the island's slaves, two of every three were African born. In time, the revolution caused class and racial fighting as "some of the whites arrayed against free blacks" on the island.[2] A significant number of white slave owners wanted to use the revolution to break away from France and establish a separate nation but still maintain slavery and white superiority as the norm. Other whites opposed their racial views and even managed to force the passage of a law on the island that granted voting privileges to some blacks. This simply ignited further clashes between the various racial factions.

At first, the black slaves on Santo Domingo were uninvolved in the conflicts, having no legal rights recognized by the French. Then, in August 1791, a massive slave revolt began to unfold, and it lead to the deaths of thousands of whites and the destruction of much property held by whites. (An uprising in the spring of that year, led by a mulatto named Jacques Vincent Oge, had been brutally crushed.) In a

This 1871 drawing shows the embarkadero, or wharf, of Santo Domingo City, which may have looked much like this when Napoleon sent his troops to the Caribbean island.

matter of weeks, the French revolutionary assembly declared equal rights for all free men, including French blacks. The institution of slavery was kept intact, however. To help subdue the violence that had racked the island for months, the French government dispatched 7,000 troops to Santo Domingo to put down the slave rebellion and enforce the new equality of all free men. This time, the uprising would not be stopped as easily. In fact, the fighting would drag on for 13 extremely violent and bloody years. Among the leaders of this 1791 rebellion was a former slave named Toussaint L'Ouverture.

BORN INTO SLAVERY

Toussaint L'Ouverture was born a slave on the island's Breda plantation in 1743. (His birth name was Francois Dominique Toussaint.) As an adult, he was good friends with one of the plantation's managers, Bayou de Libertad. Unlike most of the island's slave population, who were commonly exploited through hard labor on Santo Domingo's lucrative sugar plantations, Toussaint received some schooling and served as Libertad's coachman. He married Suzanne Simon-Baptiste and, by age 38, was granted his freedom, becoming a free man of color, who "lived as well as any former slave in St. Domingue prior to the slave revolt."[3]

Those who led the August 1791 uprising were men in a situation similar to Toussaint L'Ouverture's. They were among the most privileged of the island's black population, including slaves and former slaves who had or were working as plantation overseers, domestic servants, and coachmen, as was Toussaint. Although historians disagree over the significance of the role that Toussaint played in the events of that August, some believe it was crucial—that he helped plan the various stages of the rebellion. He was a free black, so he would have been able to travel freely from group to group. Toussaint left the Breda plantation that fall, then enlisted in the slave army marching under Generals Jean Francois and Georges Bissou. His first military duty was in service to the Spanish, who exercised control over the eastern half of Hispaniola. Over the following three years, Toussaint was probably dubbed "L'Ouverture," which some historians believe is taken from the French term for "Opening," referring to the black military leader's ability to take advantage of any break or "opening" in the enemy's line of defense. (Others think it may have been a nickname given Toussaint because of a wide gap in his front teeth.) Toussaint became an adept field commander, as well as a savvy observer of island politics. Moving up quickly in the ranks, he became third in command after Francois and Bissou. He was so recognized for his military tactics and victories that Toussaint was dubbed "Doctor of the King's Armies," "the Bonaparte of the Antilles," and "the black Napoleon."

By the spring of 1794, just a few months after the abolition of slavery by the ruling, revolutionary French body, the National Convention, driven by his own personal desire to see slavery ended on the island, the black general initially joined himself with French Governor General Étienne Laveaux, whose armies were fighting Spanish and British forces. The British had invaded Santo Domingo in 1793, during the French Revolution, thinking they could take advantage of France's internal problems. Initially, the British did well for themselves, nearly succeeding in taking control of the entire French West Indies. British fortunes changed rapidly, however. Parliament poured large sums of money into the campaign, even as 13,000 British troops lost their lives, not to the island's battlefields, but to another enemy—the mosquito. Yellow fever and malaria nearly decimated the British Redcoats.

For the next four years, Toussaint L'Ouverture and fellow rebel General André Rigaud fought in a delicate military struggle to eliminate these enemies that he and the French held in common. Slowly, they moved deftly into positions of power while working to neutralize the importance of the French on Santo Domingo. By 1796, Toussaint held so much political power that he was able to convince Laveaux to appoint him as lieutenant governor. By 1799, Toussaint and Rigaud were fighting mulatto forces on the southern portion of the island, a conflict that became known as the War of the Knives (1799–1800). Toussaint emerged from that conflict after he suppressed his mulatto opposition, even as he subdued the remaining Spanish forces. With this dual defeat of the mulattos and the Spanish, Toussaint became the true ruling power on the island.

Because Toussaint came to power largely by military means, the victorious black general built a new government on

This is a drawing of Francois-Dominique Toussaint L'Ouverture (circa 1743–1803), a Haitian patriot and former slave who led the rebellion of 1791–1803. He later was captured, charged with conspiracy, and sent to France, where he died at Fort-de-Joux.

the island, designed to bring stability to Santo Domingo, which had been racked by years of upheaval. At the same time, he managed to give himself significant power. A new framework of government, known as the Constitution of 1801, was drawn up. This document banned slavery and declared Toussaint as lifelong governor. Even Napoleon Bonaparte, France's first consul, recognized the former slave leader as captain general of Santo Domingo. Bonaparte's stamp of approval meant little to Toussaint, however. He proclaimed the new constitution to be binding and law before Bonaparte approved it. Living under the yoke of French domination was no more a part of Toussaint's game plan than living under Spanish rule or returning to his former life as a slave. His plan was to rule over a Santo Domingo independent from French control. But even as Toussaint L'Ouverture surrounded himself with power on the island of Santo Domingo, Bonaparte was making a power play of his own.

A CARIBBEAN CAMPAIGN

Robert Livingston's introduction to the world of diplomacy with the French did not present much hope to the American diplomat that he, Bonaparte, and Talleyrand would soon hammer out any agreements concerning the future of Louisiana. This, combined with Bonaparte's military intentions concerning Santo Domingo, cast doubt on any opportunity for agreement. Within just two weeks of this first meeting between the American representative and the French leader, a French fleet set sail from the natural harbor at Brest, near the entrance of the English Channel, for the New World. These vessels carried an army of thousands, mostly field-experienced Swiss and Polish conscripts, under the command of a brother-in-law of Bonaparte's, General Charles Leclerc. The general had only taken command of these forces less than two months earlier.

Leclerc's mission was twofold: (1) to put down the slave uprising on the island and restore order to Santo Domingo, and then, (2) to proceed to New Orleans and establish a permanent presence there. He was to accomplish this in three steps, according to Bonaparte's plan. First, General Leclerc was to occupy the towns along the island's coast within two or three weeks. Second, he was to attack into the interior and destroy all resistance. Third, he was to take all weapons from everyone on the island to avoid further uprisings and "destroy local leadership, so that only Frenchmen will be obeyed."[4] This was to include agreeing to give Toussaint L'Ouverture and his fellow officers anything they might ask for until the French military was in complete control of the island. Then, they were to "arrest all suspects in office whatever their color, and at the same moment embark [to France] all the black generals no matter what their conduct, patriotism, or past services."[5] A second fleet was already being formed at Dunkerque to include 4,000 additional troops under a second commander, General Claude Victor-Perrin, along with additional fleets at other French and Dutch ports.

Leclerc's fleet sailed the Atlantic without incident. The winds were decent, and the French had signed a treaty in late October, the Treaty of Amiens, that established peace on the high seas. On February 1, 1802, the ships landed off the coast of Cap François. Other fleets soon joined his, and they delivered thousands of additional troops. In time, the concerned American consul on the island, Tobias Lear, who had previously served as President Washington's personal secretary, sent a message to Federal City "that forty-six ships carrying forty thousand troops had arrived and twenty-five more ships and another twenty thousand soldiers were expected."[6] To the American observer, something big appeared to be in the wind.

As for the Americans, they had already made their position on Toussaint L'Ouverture clear. By the time Leclerc's forces landed on the island, Secretary of State James Madison had already placed Lear in the U.S. consul and the new diplomat had sent his congratulations to Toussaint as the new ruler of

Santo Domingo. When the French charge d'affaires in the U.S. capital, Louis Andre Pichon, protested, Madison assured him that he and Jefferson were still highly pro-French and that Lear only offered his support so that the black leader might not be driven to cause a slave rebellion in the United States.

LECLERC'S ARMY MARCHES

Although Bonaparte had paved the way for Leclerc by assuring Toussaint that he was pleased with him and his success on the island, the black general was immediately skeptical as more and more French ships and French troops began arriving on his island. The scope was simply too large. Then, when one of Toussaint's generals in command of Cap François, Henri Christophe, was ordered to surrender control of the harbor town, things were immediately clear. Christophe refused and even burned the port town and ordered the deaths of all white residents before abandoning his post and melting away with his forces into the island's jungles.

Suddenly, General Leclerc's position on the island was in jeopardy. Faced with a burned-out city, the French officer discovered that most of the local food supply was now onboard American ships in the harbor. He was forced to pay outrageous prices to the Americans, which caused him to immediately run low on funds. When he sent a representative to New York City to arrange a loan of one million francs, no banks in the city would provide the funds. French credit, in the aftermath of the revolution, was in a relative shambles.

Caught in a desperate situation, General Leclerc chose to seize the supplies he needed from American merchants on the island, causing a storm of protest. When the local Americans and U.S. sea captains protested, they were simply threatened with a return to the days of French seizure of American ships. Back in the States, newspapers howled in anger and vilified the French and their commander. News of the events in Santo

Domingo reached President Jefferson and James Madison by early March, and they included reports of the heavy-handed tactics of the French commander. A letter reached the president, written by a Kentuckian who had signed on as an officer in the French cavalry under Leclerc's command. In the letter, delivered by Lear, the American mercenary provided information "that a part of the French expedition was destined for Louisiana."[7]

In the meantime, French charge d'affaires Pichon was sending letters of his own, to Leclerc, reprimanding him for his actions against American interests. He also sent a letter to Talleyrand, asking the obvious: Why had a French army been dispatched to a violence-torn Caribbean island, a seedbed of rebellion, without adequate funds? Pichon himself was soon faced with difficult questions when Secretary of State Madison summoned him to explain why the French had sent so many troops to Santo Domingo and whether those troops were actually intended for duty in Louisiana. Pichon only responded that he did not know (and indeed, he did not!). When he practically begged for Madison's help in arranging the one million franc loan, "Madison stared at Pichon as if he had gone insane."[8] There would be no such loan, responded the American secretary. For a short time, Pichon was hopeful that President Jefferson might respond differently. An initial meeting with the chief executive included the American leader's promise to consult with several members of Congress, but no assistance was forthcoming. The only Americans ready to cooperate with the French diplomat, it seemed, were Federalists, Jefferson's opposition party, and they urged Pichon to take a firm stand against the president.

A CLASH OF ARMIES

As French and American representatives discussed among themselves their positions and preferences regarding French intentions on the island and in Louisiana, further fighting unfolded on Santo Domingo. That spring and summer, Leclerc's troops were embroiled in a full-scale war. After destroying Cap François, the French general captured additional strategic locations along the coast, staying on his schedule by completing his march within 10 days. Then, he prepared for jungle fighting. Once he moved into the interior, Leclerc encountered black forces under the command of one of Toussaint's top generals, Jean Jacques Dessalines. Dessalines was advancing ahead of him, killing every white islander he could find, as well as any black or mixed blood who appeared ready to cooperate with the French. By mid-February, General Leclerc targeted an important interior position of his opponent, Toussaint's stronghold at Gonaïves. Defectors from among the black island leader's ranks, including several black generals who swore their allegiance to Leclerc and joined his forces, helped Leclerc.

Touissant soon attacked, ambushing the French on February 23 at a location several miles outside Gonaïves. Success in battle was first in Leclerc's favor, then in Toussaint's, then in Leclerc's, and at one point Toussaint's troops almost routed the French. Only the actions of one of Leclerc's generals, Jean-Baptiste-Donatien de Vimeur, Count de Rochambeau, turned the tide. (Rochambeau's father had led a French army alongside General Washington during the final battle of the American Revolution at Yorktown.) As French forces appeared ready to retreat, Rochambeau threw his officer's hat back into the path of the advancing black rebels. Above the din, he shouted: "My comrades, you will not leave your general's hat behind!"[9] The gesture caused the wavering French line to turn about and face their enemy, which soon led to a rout of Toussaint L'Ouverture's men. On February 24, the French advanced into Gonaïves, setting the town on fire.

After months of fighting on the island, General Leclerc's army struggled. He lost men at an alarming rate, as many as 2,000 in a single day of fighting. French troops were dying, not just from the fighting, but from the same malady that had stopped the British in their tracks back in the early 1790s. The illness was alarming to the French general and his men:

> [F]or the first time he noticed a strange illness creeping through his army. Soldiers weakened without warning; in a day they were too sick to walk. Then came black vomit, yellowing skin, convulsions, and death. Neither Leclerc nor anyone else realized that this "yellow fever" was produced by a tiny female mosquito now known to scientists as *Aedes aegypti*.[10]

The deadly mosquito bred in every stagnant pool of water on the island. Its habitat included not only the Caribbean but also parts of South and Central America, as well as Africa. The death rate experienced by a community exposed to the ravages spread by the *Aedes aegypti* mosquito might run as high as 85 percent.

These dual diseases of yellow fever and malaria continued to plague General Leclerc's army as the weeks of fighting continued. By late April, in a letter, the French commander lamented: "I have tried several times to make Toussaint and all the generals surrender," but "I would not be able to adopt those rigorous measures which are needed to assure to France the undisputed possession of San Domingo until I have 25,000 Europeans present under arms."[11] By the end of the third week of April, 5,000 of Leclerc's forces were dead, and an additional 5,000 lay in the hospital, dying. This number totaling 10,000 men constituted well more than half of his original 17,000 troops.

There was some good news for Leclerc by the end of the month. General Henri Christophe, whom Leclerc had driven from Cap François, a few months earlier, defected to the French, along with 1,200 cavalry, who delivered 100 cannons to the French. This turn of events created a great change in the fighting. It was a loss from which Toussaint believed he could not recover. After gaining a promise of freedom for all blacks, as well as continued rank for black officers, Toussaint agreed to a truce with Leclerc on May 1 and was joined five days later by a reluctant Dessalines.

Historians have asked many times over why Toussaint surrendered, even though he had faced down the French at nearly

A TREACHEROUS ACT

Although the fighting between French forces under the command of General Leclerc and those of the island commanders sometimes led to acts of atrocity and brutality, the conflict also produced a single act of treachery that would forever mark the personal legacy of the French commander. The details tell a tale based on lies and deceit.

The capture of Toussaint was cleverly planned by Leclerc, who took advantage of his opponent's belief that a gentleman, such as the French general, would be true to his word. When Leclerc offered Toussaint a dinner invitation to a nearby plantation, he claimed to offer him free passage, stating that the engagement was needed "to discuss important matters that cannot be explained by letter."* Trusting Leclerc as a man of his word, Toussaint even refused to take along his usual complement of guards.

Toussaint L'Ouverture had been cruelly tricked. Even as he was arrested and prepared for deportation to France, the black general still believed the revolution in Santo Domingo would continue. While boarding the French frigate, *Heros*, L'Ouverture predicted the future: "In overthrowing me, you have cut down in San Domingue only the trunk of the tree of liberty. It will spring up again by the roots for they are numerous and deep."**

General Leclerc publicly explained himself to put his actions in the best possible light. On June 11, 1802, he recounted his side of these events in *Le Moniteur de la Louisiane*:

every turn. It may be that his most significant incentive came when he learned that his enemy had recently signed a peace treaty with the British at Amiens. With the French no longer distracted by the British military or navy, Bonaparte would be free to dispatch endless reinforcements to the island. Surrendering earlier rather than later would give him better terms.

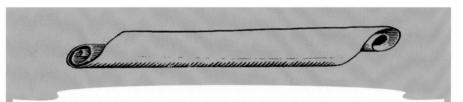

From the General in Chief to the Citizens of St. Domingue:
General Toussaint did not wish to profit from the amnesty that had been granted to him. He continued to conspire, he was going to re-ignite the civil war. I had to have him arrested. The proofs of his bad conduct after the amnesty will be repeatedly published. This measure, which assures peace in the Colony, should in no way disturb those who have turned in their arms and submitted to the good faith of the Republic.[*]

French authorities shipped the black general across the Atlantic to France, where Bonaparte placed him in a cold, damp cell in a castle in the Jura Mountains near the Swiss border, about 50 miles (80 kilometers) from Geneva. There, the unfortunate Toussaint died on April 7, 1803, of cold, neglect, and starvation. As for the French general who had treated him so treacherously, Leclerc had already died six months earlier, himself a victim of yellow fever.

---

[*]*Charles A. Cerami*, Jefferson's Great Gamble: The Remarkable Story of Jefferson, Napoleon and the Men Behind the Louisiana Purchase. *Naperville, Illw.: Sourcebooks, 2003, p. 51.*

[**]*Jon Kukla*, A Wilderness So Immense: The Louisiana Purchase and the Destiny of America. *New York: Knopf, 2003, p. 223.*

Over the next few weeks, the truce Toussaint agreed to appeared to have been premature. Leclerc's army continued to suffer under the effects of the *Aedes aegypti*. It was the rainy season, and disease continued to shrink the French general's ranks. In one report, Leclerc noted: "I have at this moment 3,600 men in hospital and no day passes without from 200 to 250 men entering the hospitals, while not more than 50 come out."[12] That May, 3,000 French soldiers died. In one unfortunate regiment that had originally landed on the island with nearly 1,400 men, the number of survivors was reduced to 190 soldiers. Something would have to be done to ensure that Toussaint did not have the opportunity to renounce his truce. Inviting the black general to sit down and discuss matters in person, Leclerc was able to fool Toussaint and arrest him. By June, the rebel leader was shipped to France, where he died only months later.

"Embryo of a Tornado"

With the elimination of "the Black Napoleon" from Santo Domingo, events soon took a dramatic turn. By fall, General Leclerc himself died of yellow fever, and command of his forces on the island shifted to General Rochambeau. Americans could recall Rochambeau's father's contribution to the American Revolution (he aided the victory at Yorktown more than 20 years earlier), but the son was not the father. Leclerc had fought a limited war, but Rochambeau prepared to carry out a harsh, destructive policy against his enemies. In a letter, he wrote, "To regain St. Domingue," France "must send hither 25,000 men in a body, declare the negroes slaves, and destroy at least 30,000 negroes and negresses—the latter being more cruel than the men. These measures are frightful, but necessary. We must take them or renounce the colony."[1]

A NEW COMMANDER

Rochambeau soon began implementing his racist policies of extermination. He ordered 16 of Toussaint's captured officers chained to a rock in Cap Francais's harbor to die of exposure and starvation. The last one died after 17 agonizing days. Another rebel general was lashed to a ship's mast. As French soldiers "nailed his epaulettes to his bare shoulders," he was forced to witness the drowning of his wife and children.[2] For a solid year, the carnage on the island reached titanic levels. French soldiers chained their black victims together like slaves, then drowned them. Many were torn apart by dogs. The bodies of hanged islanders were a constant reminder of the harsh retributions meted out by Rochambeau. There were atrocities on both sides. By November 1803, Bonaparte's dream of establishing control of Santo Domingo was shattered. He had lost 60,000 troops to the fighting and the dual scourges of yellow fever and malaria. The French had killed off more than a third of a million Haitians, including blacks, whites, and mulattos. Toussaint's prediction that his capture would only cause the roots of liberty to flourish had proven correct. His second in command, General Dessalines, had engaged in a furious campaign to drive the French into the sea. By the end of the month, Rochambeau and his bedraggled army abandoned the island. Weeks later, on January 1, 1804, the islanders established the free Republic of Haiti.

A CHANGE OF PERSPECTIVE

The removal of Toussaint L'Ouverture from the complicated chess board of Santo Domingo by the late spring of 1802 was a stunning turn of events for President Jefferson. It had happened so quickly, so unexpectedly. He even wondered if the information he received had not actually been the opposite; that Leclerc had surrendered and that the French would soon abandon the Caribbean island. This latest development would lead to another, one directly affecting the United States. The same day Dessalines surrendered, on May 6, 1802, the American diplomat on the island, Tobias Lear, appeared in Federal City and made an unannounced call on Secretary of State Madison. Lear explained he had been removed from his post by General Leclerc and sent packing. Lear had made a sharp point concerning the imprisonment of two American sea captains, one of whom had been arrested simply for having reported on the bloody takeover of Cap François by the French. Lear carried yet another message, however. He had spoken with French officers who told him that the French Revolution was over, that their country's experiment with republicanism had run its course, and that Bonaparte would soon take the old Bourbon throne as a new French monarch. This, perhaps, disappointed Jefferson more than the rest of Lear's report. He had been in Paris in the summer of 1789 when the revolution had broken out, with all its hopes of freedom and constitutional rule. He had supported the revolution and had remained a cautious associate of Bonaparte's. No more, though. Jefferson's love of all things French immediately came crashing in.

Jefferson's attachment to France had, in fact, already begun to crack. The real sticking point concerning Santo Domingo had never really been about French control of a Caribbean island, as such. The worry for the United States had always been the possible transfer of Louisiana to France and an aggressive French effort to reestablish a New World empire, and the Americans were not sitting still waiting around for events to overtake them.

DIPLOMATIC EXCHANGES

Back in France, U.S. Minister Robert Livingston pushed for another meeting with Foreign Minister Talleyrand. Livingston even asked Talleyrand directly if Spain had returned Louisiana to France. Talleyrand denied it. Livingston tried to negotiate with the powerful French minister. He offered to drop $5 million in American claims against France that had not been covered in the Treaty of Mortefontaine, which settled damages related to the Quasi-War. The American minister offered to drop the claims altogether in exchange for West Florida and the port of New Orleans. Talleyrand rebuffed the offer outright, stating: "None but spendthrifts satisfy their debts by selling their lands," which he followed with a pause and added: "But it is not ours to give."[3] Livingston then made another offer to the French. The United States would like to buy all of Louisiana north of the confluence of the Arkansas and Mississippi Rivers. This would leave New Orleans in French hands and place the Americans as a buffer between the British in Canada and the French to the south. Again, Talleyrand refused the suggestion.

In fact, Talleyrand was technically telling Livingston the truth. The Spanish monarch, King Carlos IV, had not signed documents that would transfer Louisiana to France, and a significant group of Spanish court officials, led by the former foreign minister, Manuel de Godoy, was opposed to the transfer. What Talleyrand did not tell Livingston was that Napoleon Bonaparte was growing tired of the Spanish putting him off. He had even informed his ambassador to the Spanish court to tell Godoy that "if this system [of delay] is continued . . . it will terminate in a thunderbolt."[4] Even as Talleyrand insisted the transfer of Louisiana was not in the cards, though, everywhere in Paris the talk was of the retroceding of the lands watered by the vast Mississippi River Valley. Livingston heard of it on the streets, in the gossipy salons in Paris, in newspapers and in books. He told Madison: "Louisiana is a very favorite measure here."[5]

Even before the surrender of Toussaint L'Ouverture in the spring of 1802, President Jefferson began to step up his efforts to "discourage Napoleon" from taking control of Louisiana.[6] The American leader wanted to make it clear to the French leader that he did not want the two countries to become close neighbors. He made his intentions clear to Robert Livingston when he sat down and wrote a letter to the American minister on

April 18, 1802. The communication "is surely one of the most emotional letters ever written by an American president."[7]

Fortunately, Jefferson was able to find a proper and trustworthy courier for his letter to Livingston. Pierre Samuel du Pont de Nemours was the president's friend, and he fled France during the latter years of the revolution. He and his family established a gunpowder factory in Delaware. To du Pont, Jefferson expressed his belief that, should France take Louisiana as her own, it "will cost France, and perhaps not very long hence, a war which will annihilate her on the ocean."[8] Although the annexation of Louisiana might appear to be a small thing in the larger scheme of European affairs, the president warned that "this little event" that "now appears as an almost invisible point in the horizon, is the embryo of a tornado which will burst on the countries on both sides of the Atlantic and involve in its effect their highest destinies."[9]

As for the letter Jefferson entrusted to du Pont, it was straightforward, detailed, and to the point:

> The cession of Louisiana and the Floridas by Spain to France works most sorely on the United States. This subject the Secretary of State has written to you fully, yet I cannot forbear recurring to it personally, so deep is the impression it makes on my mind. It completely reverses all the political relations of the United States, and will form a new epoch in our political course. Of all nations of any consideration, France is the one which, hitherto, has offered the fewest points on which we could have any conflict of right, and the most points of a communion of interests.... Her growth, therefore, we viewed as our own, her misfortunes ours. There is on the globe one single spot, the possessor of which is our natural and habitual enemy. It is New Orleans, through which the produce of three-eighths of our territory must pass to market, and from its fertility it will ere long yield more than half of our whole produce and contain more than half of our inhabitants. France, placing herself in that door, assumes

**Pierre du Pont de Nemours (1739–1817) was a French econo-
mist. He was also a friend to President Thomas Jefferson, and
he agreed to deliver the president's letter to Robert Livingston,
thus beginning the negotiations for the Louisiana Purchase.**

to us the attitude of defiance. Spain might have retained
it quietly for years. . . . Not so can it ever be in the hands
of France: The impetuosity of her temper, the energy and
restlessness of her character, placed in a point of eternal
friction with us.[10]

Having recast the future relationship between the United States and France in the case of the retrocession of Louisiana, President Jefferson then continued the letter, stating that the transfer from Spain to France would:

> Render it impossible that France and the United States can continue long friends. . . . They, as well as we, must be blind if they do not see this; and we must be very improvident if we do not begin to make arrangements on that hypothesis.
>
> The day that France takes possession of New Orleans, fixes the sentence which is to restrain her forever within her low-water mark. It seals the union of two nations, who, in conjunction, can maintain exclusive possession of the ocean. From that moment, we must marry ourselves to the British fleet and nation . . . and having formed and connected together a power which may render reinforcement of her settlements here impossible to France, make the first cannon which shall be fired in Europe the signal for the tearing up [of] any settlement she may have made, and for holding the two continents of America in sequestration for the common purposes of the United British and American nations.[11]

Here is a frustrated President Jefferson, who had remained a Francophile for so many years, as he is forced to abandon any thoughts of continuing a friendship with France. He is even driven by the circumstances to consider an alliance of the United States with Great Britain, in order to rely on its powerful navy. The situation was not ideal, as Jefferson further noted: "This is not a state of things we seek or desire," but "it is one which this measure, if adopted by France, forces on us."[12] Louisiana was simply too important. "Every eye in the U.S. is now fixed on this affair of Louisiana," the president had written.[13]

Even as Jefferson blustered on paper about the possible transfer of Louisiana to France, there was really little he or his secretary of state could do about it. Madison himself sent another letter on May 1 to Livingston, expressing his own frustrations. Louisiana, he wrote, "becomes daily more and more a source of painful apprehensions."[14] Livingston's own letters written back to Jefferson and Madison were just as gloomy. In one, he wrote that "no hope remains" that France might not take back Louisiana. Everything was falling into Bonaparte's lap. He was poised to annex Louisiana, knowing that only a weak Spanish king stood in his way. The march toward retrocession seemed assured. (The official transfer of Louisiana to the French took place on October 25, 1802, as King Carlos IV of Spain signed the royal order.)

A STONE IN THE RIVER

Throughout the summer of 1802, the situation regarding the possession of Louisiana changed little. Toussaint L'Ouverture was gone, and the fighting in Santo Domingo continued with a ferocious and bloody intensity. French troops continued to drop like flies, sometimes at the rate of more than 100 a day. Livingston continued to work on negotiations to purchase New Orleans and West Florida, but Talleyrand simply kept him off balance, refusing to agree to anything and continuing to deny France's true intentions.

Then on October 16, 1802, a lifelong Spanish bureaucrat, one who took his first job at age 12 as a customs clerk, 46-year-old Juan Ventura Morales, who was then serving as intendant (governor) of New Orleans, "hurled a stone into the Mississippi"[15] and announced the closing of the port to American trade that reached the city by way of the Mississippi River. In his own words, "From this date the privilege which the Americans had of importing and depositing their merchandise and effects in this capital, shall be interdicted."[16] Since taking on his role as acting intendant at New Orleans in 1796, Morales had proven himself to be a controversial figure and antagonistic toward the United States. Morales's announcement came with almost no warning. News of his decision spread quickly up the Mississippi River, reaching Natchez in just two days and leapfrogging its way north to settlements along the Ohio River, in Kentucky, and beyond, even to Washington City. Some reports of what was happening in New Orleans conflicted. By one account, Kentucky farmers were having their flatboats of cotton turned away from the port by Spanish officials. Other reports stated that such western flatboats were being allowed to deposit their cargoes by paying a customs duty. Newspapers from Kentucky to Maryland blasted the Spanish. The pages of American papers spoke of future conflict between the Americans and Spanish, with one paper "fully expecting a war."[17]

It was the denial of the "right of deposit" that had driven the fears of westerners for years. The United States had negotiated an agreement with Spain, back in 1795, known as Pinckney's Treaty, that had guaranteed the American right of deposit in New Orleans for three years. After 1798, the Spanish could continue the right and Spanish officials, including Morales, had done so. Suddenly, however, the intendant had decided that continuing to allow Americans to use the port by depositing their trade goods in warehouses in New Orleans until they were exported out was a "direct and open violation of the treaty," which Morales insisted could not be continued "without an express order of the King."[18]

Word of the closing of New Orleans to American river traffic reached the U.S. capital five weeks later. Rather than panic, President Jefferson and Secretary of State Madison expressed their hope that the decision had been made by Morales alone, without any input from higher Spanish officials. By assuming so, Jefferson was providing wriggle room for Spain to rescind the decision, even if it had been made by King Carlos IV himself. Nevertheless, Jefferson and Madison looked on the development with great concern. As Madison would soon write, taking away the right of deposit "is so direct and palpable a violation of the Treaty of 1795 that in candor it is to be imputed rather to the Intendant solely, than to instructions of his Government."[19]

Other Spanish officials backed up Madison's hope. The Spanish ambassador in Washington City informed Madison that Morales had, indeed, gone beyond his own authority. Reports that the Spanish governor of Louisiana had not played any role in the decision were also encouraging to the Americans.

Sorting all that out was not that important to Madison or Jefferson, however. What *was* important was that the decision not stand. In a communication from the secretary of state to Charles Cotesworth Pinckney, the American diplomat to Spain, "the President expects that the Spanish Government will neither lose a moment in countermanding it, nor hesitate to repair every damage which may result from it."[20] Madison understood the gravity of the situation. The closing of the port had angered and upset many Americans, especially those located on the western frontiers between the Appalachians and the Mississippi. That anger, he wrote

> is justified by the interest they have at stake. The Mississippi is to them every thing. It is the Hudson, the Delaware, the Potomac, and all the navigable rivers of the atlantic states formed into one stream. The produce exported through that channel last year amounted to $1,622,672 from the districts of Kentucky and Mississippi [alone], and will probably be fifty per cent more this year . . . a great part of which is now or shortly will be afloat for New Orleans and consequently exposed to the effects of this extraordinary exercise of power.[21]

Indeed, westerners were upset. When Madison soon met with the French charge d'affaires, Louis Andre Pichon, he warned him that anything might happen when the estimated 5,000 or 6,000 Americans floating their wares down the Mississippi were denied the right of deposit in New Orleans. As fellow Kentuckian Robert Barr wrote to one of his state senators, John

King Carlos IV of Spain (1748–1819) was the reigning monarch during the time of Spain's interest in Louisiana.

Breckinridge, "all ready and waiting to step on board and sail down and take possession of New Orleans."[22]

A ROYAL DECISION

Even as Jefferson and Madison hoped against hope that the decision to close New Orleans had been made only by some low-level bureaucrat such as Morales, the fact was that the decision had been issued from the pinnacle of Spanish authority. The order was actually issued by the Spanish monarch Carlos IV himself three months earlier, on July 14. The king's decision was based on reports from Spanish officials, including Morales, who claimed that "Americans were abusing the right of deposit and heavily engaged in smuggling."[23] King Carlos, directly under the advice of his chief minister, Pedro de Cevallos, who had replaced Manuel Godoy, had made the decision secretly, instructing Morales to make the announcement regarding the port closing, while telling him not to do so in the name of the king. Morales was to pretend he was making the decision on his interpretation of the tenets of Pinckney's Treaty. The Spanish intendant followed King Carlos IV's instructions to the letter, and the monarch escaped immediate blame. In fact, his decision remained a secret for the next century, only to be realized by a twentieth-century historian named Edward Channing.

As for the decision, whether made by Morales or Carlos IV, Napoleon Bonaparte, who received word in January, 1803, could not have been happier. Continued American access to New Orleans did not fit the First Consul's plan for dominating Louisiana. He and his ministers "welcomed Morales's proclamation as a measure that would curb American competitors and encourage French commerce."[24]

The path to French dominance over Louisiana was not yet paved with ease. The war between the French and rebel islanders had become bogged down. Mosquitoes continued to thin the ranks of Bonaparte's army. The French leader then received word in January 1803 of General Leclerc's death in November.

Napoleon Bonaparte's dreams of a New World empire based on the lucrative profits of the sugar trade were teetering on the brink of disaster. Like Jefferson and Madison, he, too, was struggling over Louisiana. Yes, by secret arrangement, the French already *owned* New Orleans. Taking true, actual control of the region remained elusive, however—and Napoleon's reach exceeded his grasp. His frustrations exploded following a formal dinner party held on January 12, 1803, when he went into a tirade, shouting: "Damn sugar, damn coffee, damn colonies!"[25]

Meanwhile, pressure was mounting in the United States. Through the spring of 1803, more and more people called for military action against the Spanish. In March, Senator James Ross of Pennsylvania delivered a bill to the floor that handed Jefferson $5 million in funding and the authority to raise an army of 50,000 to march against and capture New Orleans. Continuing to press Bonaparte at every opportunity to bargain with his country over Louisiana, Livingston made certain that the French leader received a copy of the *New York Chronicle,* which published Ross's congressional proposals, including his call for a punitive force of 50,000. When word of the bill reached Pichon, the French official was outraged. He soon took it upon himself to publish a letter in which he boldly claimed that his government did not approve of the closing of New Orleans to Americans, even though Bonaparte was actually delighted by the move. Such actions merely confused U.S. government officials about what the closing of the port at the mouth of the Mississippi really meant to anyone except American citizens.

What anxious, saber-rattling Americans could not know with certainly was that Napoleon Bonaparte was already considering selling Louisiana and ridding himself of the failures it represented for the first consul's dreams of an empire in North America. Santo Domingo had cost millions of francs, and the general was eyeing other military ventures, including the retaking of Egypt. That spring, Bonaparte began preparing for a

(continues on page 82)

BONAPARTES IN THE BATHROOM

By the early 1800s, Napoleon Bonaparte was the undisputed leader of France. Although he was one of the most powerful political figures in European history, he also relied heavily on support, especially from his brothers and sisters. (General Leclerc had been married to one of Bonaparte's sisters.) With his siblings often close by, the French leader could use them as listening boards, bouncing his intentions off them for perspective. When he made his decision to divest himself of Louisiana, several of his brothers weighed in and expressed their concerns and disapproval. The story is told of one such encounter among the Bonaparte brothers in a bathroom where Napoleon was taking a bath.

As the story goes, two of Napoleon's brothers, Lucien and Joseph, were upset with his plans to sell Louisiana, and they decided to confront their brother directly. Both men paid a visit to Bonaparte's palace in Paris, the Tuileries, where they found him in the bathroom taking a bath in a tub of rosewater. (The Tuileries was torn down in 1871 and is now the site of the modern glass pyramid that stands beside the Louvre.) Before either sibling brought up the issue, Napoleon asked them what they thought about his intent to give up Louisiana. Lucien spoke up, repeating what he had already rumored: That his brother was going to give up Louisiana without consulting the approval of the French parliament (called the Chamber).

"I flatter myself," said Lucien, "that the Chambers will not give their consent."

Napoleon, still in the tub, responded caustically: "You flatter yourself. That is precious, in truth."

"And I flatter myself," Joseph, the third Bonaparte brother, added, "as I have already told the First Consul."

"And what did I answer?" scowled Napoleon.

"That you would do without the Chambers," answered Joseph.

At that point, Napoleon began to mock his brothers, informing them he did not need their approval or that of the Chamber to sell Louisiana.

An angry Joseph then approached Napoleon's bathtub, telling him he would directly defy his powerful brother and lead the opposition against ridding France of Louisiana without the proper approvals. Napoleon only laughed: "You will have no need to lead the opposition, for I repeat that there will be no debate."

Napoleon then stood up in the tub and angrily lit into his brothers: "It is my idea. I conceived it, and I shall go through with it, the negotiation, ratification, and execution, by myself. Do you understand? By me who scoffs at your opposition."

An equally angry Joseph began shouting back at his brother, and, as the tirades rose, Napoleon, done with the conversation, shouted out: "You are insolent!" then fell back into his tub, throwing a great wave of rosy water all over his insulted and incensed brothers.

Wet, but quick with his response, Lucien then quoted from Virgil's Roman classic, *Aeneid*: "I will show you . . . ! But no, first I had better set the waves at rest; after that you are going to pay dearly for your offence."

The argument had become so heated that Napoleon's valet fainted dead away, even as the trio of Bonapartes tried to calm themselves.

A soaked Joseph then left the room to change into dry clothes. It was then that Napoleon spoke to Lucien in a resigned voice of confession: "Do you want me to tell you the truth? I am today more sorry than I like to confess for the expedition to St. Domingue." It had cost

(continues)

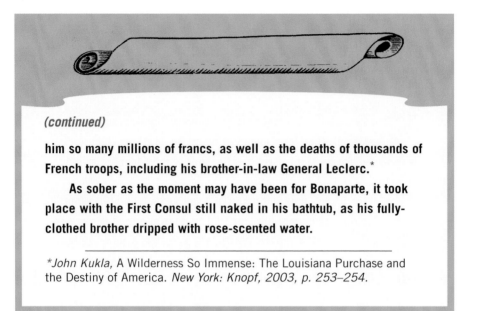

(continued)

him so many millions of francs, as well as the deaths of thousands of French troops, including his brother-in-law General Leclerc.[*]

As sober as the moment may have been for Bonaparte, it took place with the First Consul still naked in his bathtub, as his fully-clothed brother dripped with rose-scented water.

---

[*]*John Kukla,* A Wilderness So Immense: The Louisiana Purchase and the Destiny of America. *New York: Knopf, 2003, p. 253–254.*

(continued from page 79)

new war, one he would wage not on an island in the Caribbean but on Old World battlefields. It would be an expensive war, one costing millions of francs—money, in fact, that the French treasury did not have. Bonaparte and his country had already been at war for 15 years, and the cost had been enormous. When the French leader finally made his decision to rid himself of Louisiana, it was mid-March 1803. Bonaparte also made another decision at that moment: He would not have Talleyrand negotiate an agreement with the Americans. Talleyrand, after all, did not approve of surrendering Louisiana. Bonaparte, instead, would utilize the talents of someone he could more readily trust, his finance minister, François Barbé-Marbois, a French official, unlike Talleyrand, who was considered to be both honest and incorruptible.

A NEW FRENCH NEGOTIATOR

Bonaparte's decision to offer the vast Mississippi River Valley, the great interior that stretched from the river to the Rockies, was finally made on April 10, 1803. That day, following

Mass on Easter Sunday, he called two French ministers into his chambers in the palace at St. Cloud for a serious discussion. Denis Decrès was his country's minister of marine and colonies. François Barbé-Marbois was his minister of finance. Both men ranked among the best in service to Bonaparte. Rear Admiral Decrès, a well-schooled aristocrat from Champagne, had proven himself in the military while serving under Admiral François Joseph Paul de Grasse in the West Indies (It was de Grasse's fleet that had kept the British navy from entering the Chesapeake Bay during the last big battle of the American Revolution at Yorktown, while Generals Washington and Rochambeau defeated British General Cornwallis.) The tenacious and hard-edged Decrès was also known for having broken through a British blockade at Malta during Bonaparte's march across Egypt during the 1790s. For his naval service, Bonaparte had given him a rare tribute for a naval man: He presented him with a sword of honor. Over the previous two years, he had worked closely with the many fleets sent off to the fighting on Santo Domingo. Most recently, he had sketched out strategies for a possible French invasion against Great Britain. He was a stalwart and loyal servant to Napoleon Bonaparte. At 42, he was eight years older than the first consul.

Barbé-Marbois was a man of many interests. He loved literature and was fascinated with the science of his day. He was a career diplomat by instinct, however. In him, Bonaparte had someone who could not only negotiate with the Americans, but who also had genuine affection for them. He had traveled out onto the American frontier, which included tromping along upstate New York's Mohawk River, where, one day, the Erie Canal would be constructed. In the early 1780s, during the last years of the American Revolutionary War, Barbé-Marbois had served in Philadelphia as the secretary of the French legation and later became the charge d'affaires. He was familiar with and had at one time or another worked alongside Robert Livingston, John Jay, and James Monroe. At the end of the Revolutionary War, he married an American, Elizabeth Moore, the daughter of the president of the Executive Council of Pennsylvania. He understood Bonaparte's desire to sell Louisiana. He had, after all, served for four years as the French intendant in Santo Domingo under King Louis XVI.

Like Bonaparte, Barbé-Marbois had at first supported the French Revolution, when it began in 1789. He was a moderate, however, and, as the revolution turned increasingly radical, he ran afoul of its darker elements and was first exiled then placed in prison by the Directory for more than two years in the South American colony of French Guiana. Once more moderate forces took control of the revolution, he returned to France, and, by 1801, had been placed in charge of the national treasury. Bonaparte relied on him and would continue to rely on him for years to follow. Barbé-Marbois was "a man of talents and integrity."[26] For Bonaparte, there was also one other factor qualifying Barbé-Marbois to help negotiate about Louisiana: He was not Talleyrand, whom the first consul had come to distrust.

As the three men sat down at their first discussion regarding Louisiana, Bonaparte made it clear how conflicted he was concerning the great Mississippi River Valley region. "I know the full value of Louisiana," he told them, "and I have been desirous of repairing the fault of the French negotiator who abandoned it in 1763."[27] He also understood the geography and politics of the early nineteenth century. How could he possibly anticipate holding on to Louisiana given the situation in Santo Domingo, where "our affairs . . . have been growing worse every day since the death of Leclerc."?[28] In addition, there was the constant threat of the British Navy which, even at that moment, had 20 ships in the Gulf of Mexico alone. Not only could he not expect to keep Louisiana much longer, but he also could not imagine letting it fall into the hands of the British. It was then that he spoke words both bitter and pragmatic: "I think of ceding it to the United States." Then, he added: "[The Americans] only ask of me one town in Louisiana, but I already consider the colony as entirely lost."[29]

The Negotiations Begin

Even as Bonaparte explained the situation to his knowledgeable advisers, he was practically repeating arguments for selling Louisiana to the Americans that Livingston had been making for years. As he continued, Livingston's words hung on Bonaparte's: "[I]n the hands of this growing power (the Americans), [Louisiana] will be more useful to the policy and even to the commerce of France, than if it should attempt to keep it."[1]

A CHANGE OF POLICY

Barbé-Marbois was hardly prepared to argue with Bonaparte, his reasoning, or his decision. Barbé-Marbois soon picked up where Bonarparte left off. "We should not hesitate to make a sacrifice of that which is . . . slipping from us," the finance minister agreed. "War with England is inevitable; shall we be able with very inferior naval forces to defend Louisiana against that power? . . . Can we restore fortifications that are in ruins, and construct a long chain of forts upon a frontier of four hundred leagues [1,200 miles, or 1,931 kilometers]?"[2] As finance minister, he was able to argue that the cost of Louisiana would be too high. The French had colonized the region along the Mississippi for more than a century, noted Barbé-Marbois, and yet French control of Louisiana was still tenuous at best.

As strongly as Barbé-Marbois agreed with Bonaparte's decision regarding Louisiana, Rear Admiral Decrès was not convinced. He stated that, at least to date, France was not at war with England and that Louisiana had only recently been officially handed off to the French. If the peace between England and France continues, Decrès argued, then ridding ourselves of Louisiana might appear as a "premature act of ill-founded apprehension."[3]

With significant insight, the admiral noted the extreme importance of Louisiana, both at present and in the future. No other city in the world had the potential of New Orleans. It was well on its way to becoming one of the most important ports, not just in North America, but in the world. "The Mississippi does not reach there till it has received twenty other rivers," the admiral explained, "most of which surpass in size the finest rivers of Europe."[4] As to the future, he imagined the day when a canal might be constructed across the Isthmus of Panama and connect the two mighty oceans. When that happens, he said, Louisiana "will be on this new route, and it will then be . . . of inestimable value."[5] Even if Santo Domingo is lost to France, Decrès said hopefully, "Louisiana will take its place."[6]

With both ministers having weighed in on the subject of Louisiana, Bonaparte ended the meeting, and the trio departed for the evening to their individual rooms. The next morning, April 11, the first consul summoned Barbé-Marbois. He had made up his mind:

Here, Bonaparte is depicted discussing with Talleyrand and Barbé-Marbois the treaty that would seal the Louisiana Purchase.

Irresolution and deliberation are no longer in season. I renounce Louisiana. It is not only New Orleans that I will cede, it is the whole colony without any reservation. I know the price of what I abandon, and I have sufficiently proved the importance that I attach to this province. . . . I renounce it with the greatest regret. To attempt obstinately to retain it would be folly.[7]

Then, he gave his finance minister specific instructions, and the French leader appeared to be in a hurry. Perhaps he wanted the deal over Louisiana struck before he might change his mind. "I direct you to negotiate this affair with the envoys of the United States. . . . Have an interview this very day with Mr. Livingston." Bonaparte then set his price, ordering Barbé-Marbois to ask for 50 million francs. Then, he explained what he intended to do with the money: "I require money to make war on the richest nation of the world."[8]

Then, Napoleon Bonaparte gazed into his own crystal ball, just as Decrès had done the previous day: "In two or three centuries, the Americans may be found too powerful for Europe . . . but my foresight does not embrace such remote fears. . . . It is to prevent the danger, to which the colossal power of England exposes us, that I would provide a remedy."[9]

MONROE ENTERS THE PICTURE

Once Bonaparte finally made up his mind to divest France of Louisiana, his decision aligned with other developments taking place at that time. A new American representative sent directly to Paris by President Jefferson had just arrived in the French port city of Le Havre on April 8. By April 12, he would reach Paris. His name was James Monroe.

President Jefferson sent James Monroe to France that spring with the title "envoy extraordinary." Monroe had been to France before; he served as the American ambassador during the 1790s, a post he left in 1796. During the years that followed, no one served in his place. The French government during the late 1790s was the Directory, and the five-person committee refused to recognize Charles Cotesworth Pinckney from South Carolina. Now, Monroe was being dispatched back to France on a highly secret mission.

There was one other development that paralleled Bonaparte's decision. On April 10, the very day Napoleon Bonaparte first met with ministers Decrès and Barbé-Marbois to discuss the sale of Louisiana, Talleyrand had already made an unauthorized offer of his own to Robert Livingston.

Talleyrand's "offer" to Livingston was, obviously, unofficial, even though he had summoned the American diplomat to his private residence on the Rue du Bac. A surprised Livingston had responded with a "No," even as he reminded Talleyrand that the United States had always expressed an interest in New Orleans and West Florida. The French minister explained that, if the French no longer possessed New Orleans, the remainder of Louisiana would have no real value to France. For the sake of the argument, Talleyrand asked, what might the Americans agree to pay for the whole of Louisiana? Livingston, intrigued by the question and Talleyrand's insistence on continuing the offer, replied without knowing what might be acceptable, either to the French or even to President Jefferson. Twenty million francs, he said to the French foreign minister, then equal to approximately $4 million. Talleyrand responded clearly: The offer was too low.

He then sent Livingston out, telling him to think about another offer and let him know the following day. The American diplomat then told Talleyrand that another American envoy, James Monroe, had reached the port at La Havre, that Monroe was on his way to Paris. Livingston said he would rather wait and discuss the matter with his new associate, who might have news from Washington City and President Jefferson. Only then, would it be reasonable to continue any dialogue regarding Louisiana's future. Oh, well, shrugged Talleyrand. He was not authorized to discuss Louisiana anyway. He had only been testing the waters. (It is likely that Talleyrand already knew that Bonaparte had decided to sell Louisiana and might also have known that the first consul had cut him out of the potential deal making. Quizzing Livingston may have simply been the French minister's sly way of keeping his hand in the game.) Regardless, Monroe was on his way to Paris.

Monroe's governorship of Virginia had ended on Christmas Day 1802, and just two weeks later he received a dispatch from President Jefferson. It read: "I have but a moment to inform you that the fever into which the western mind is thrown by the affair at N[ew] Orleans . . . threatens to overbear

our peace." Monroe was at that moment packing for a trip to
New York, during which his wife and daughters planned to
visit her parents while Monroe and a close friend, Senator John
Breckinridge of Kentucky, intended to inspect some properties
the senator owned on the frontier. Monroe had already put in
two decades of public service and he "was looking forward to
opening a law practice in Richmond, settling his debts, and

"TELEGRAPHING" MONROE'S ARRIVAL

When President Jefferson dispatched his good friend and civil servant
James Monroe to Paris to meet up with Robert Livingston and negotiate with the French for Louisiana, timing became crucial. Events
began to move quickly, and timely communication mattered. Even a
day's difference in receiving information might make all the difference
in what one might agree to regarding Louisiana. On one significant
occasion, a new technology helped to inform Robert Livingston of the
arrival of Monroe in France sooner than would normally happen.

When Monroe reached the French port of Le Havre on his diplomatic mission, Robert Livingston was in Paris. Livingston knew
Monroe was to arrive soon, but did not know the exact day. Monroe
knew he must get word to Livingston as quickly as possible. To that
end, he had made an acquaintance with another passenger onboard
the *Richmond* who was scheduled to make his way to the French
capital immediately after landing. Monroe decided to give him a
note to deliver to Livingston informing him of his arrival at Le Havre
and of his plan to rest a day, then proceed to Paris. The newly
arrived diplomat might not have even bothered.

Already, word of Monroe's arrival on the French coast had
reached Paris, a distance of 100 miles (161 kilometers) inland.
How was that possible, when the trip required at least a couple of

making some money."[10] Jefferson's letter now stood in the way of those plans, however.

The president wanted Monroe. His letter continued:

> I shall tomorrow nominate you to the Senate for an extraordinary mission to France and the circumstances are such as to render it impossible to decline. The whole public hope

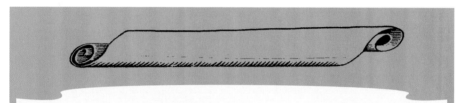

days of travel on horseback? The answer was a new communication system called the semaphore telegraph.

The system, invented by French engineer Claude Happe, dated back only a decade. It was based on a series of signal towers, each within sight of another. Chappe's "optical telegraph" involved "a semaphore with three arms that could be placed in a combination of ninety-two discrete positions."* By creating a coded vocabulary of 92 pages, each featuring 92 semaphore combinations, for a total of 8,500 words, messages could be instantly sent from tower to tower, covering the 100 miles (161 kilometers) between the port and Paris in a matter of hours rather than days.

All this allowed word of Monroe's arrival to reach Livingston, as well as Bonaparte, almost immediately. Livingston was even able to send a message back to Monroe letting him know he would expect to see him soon. As for Monroe's note to Livingston, he received it on April 10. During these busy days between April 8 and April 12, the semaphore telegraph may have influenced the course of American history.

---

*Jon Kukla, A Wilderness So Immense: The Louisiana Purchase and the Destiny of America. *New York: Knopf, 2003, p. 266.*

will be rested on you. I wish you to [stay] either in Richmond or Albemarle till you receive another letter from me,
which will be written two days hence if the Senate decide
immediately. . . . In the meantime pray work night and day
to arrange your affairs for a temporary absence; perhaps for
a long time.[11]

Both houses of Congress were, indeed, open for business
on January 11, and the work of both directly related to James
Monroe. The Senate was considering Monroe as the country's
special envoy to France and Spain. As for the House, they were
quietly meeting in secret session to earmark $2 million to pay
for "any expenses which may be incurred in relations to the
intercourse between the United States and foreign nations,"[12]
an indirect reference to Spain and France, and, perhaps, Great
Britain. Everything was proceeding in support of the purchase
of New Orleans and West Florida from France.

The resulting Senate vote broke down along party lines,
but Monroe's appointment was accepted on January 12, and
the House funding received approval the next day. On the
January 13, Jefferson told Monroe of his confirmation. The
Jefferson administration considered Monroe a valuable asset
regarding any future deals with France over Louisiana. Monroe was strong in his support of westerners and their interests
along the Mississippi River Valley. He was a western landowner
himself. He was also a veteran of dealing diplomatically with
the French and could move easily in French social circles, being
familiar with "the salons and officials of Paris from his days as
President Washington's minister, and he had friends among the
French republicans."[13] He did bring a couple of liabilities. For
one, many of his earlier French friends were not necessarily
friends or supporters of Bonaparte. He was also considered an
extremely proud, even vain man. It might have been difficult
for such a man not to have high thoughts of himself when his

A new American representative sent directly to Paris by President Jefferson had just arrived in the French port city of Le Havre on April 8. By April 12, he would reach Paris. His name was James Monroe (above).

friend, the president of the United States, was telling him: "All eyes, all hopes, are now fixed on you."[14]

With the way cleared for Monroe to sail to Paris and attach himself to Livingston and his efforts regarding Louisiana, Jefferson's instructions to him were the same as he had stated to Livingston already. He wanted New Orleans and West Florida, which would allow the United States to control the Mississippi River and other rivers that flowed into the Gulf of Mexico. As he did with Livingston, the president granted Monroe "full and frequent oral communications" regarding negotiations over Louisiana. Jefferson informed Monroe that the context of any deal-making with the French might change direction so suddenly that as a negotiator, Monroe needed to be flexible. Given that, Jefferson said, "no [written] instructions could be squared to fit them."[15] By January 13, Monroe was onboard with the project, having cancelled his plans for New York and his western venture. He locked up his law office and began making plans to sail to France.

The Diplomatic
Game Continues

The ship bearing James Monroe, Jefferson's envoy extraordinary, toward his rendezvous with American history arrived in port on April 8, a Friday. He arrived in Paris four days later, on April 12, to meet with his diplomatic partner, Robert Livingston. Together the two American negotiators could make a formidable team to face the difficulties of negotiating with the French. Even as Livingston received word that the recently arrived Monroe was on his way to Paris, the New Yorker was not exactly ecstatic. He had spent two years in the French capital, engaging in a constant dance of deferment with Talleyrand, trying his best to make a deal about Louisiana, but finding only constant frustration and rebuff. He had jousted with the best, including Talleyrand and Bonaparte. Still, he had failed thus far, and now another negotiator would soon arrive, one selected specially by President Jefferson. This new man on the scene would not simply serve as a new bargaining partner; Monroe, 15 years younger than Livingston, was arriving in Paris as his new boss.

A POSSIBLE OFFER

To complicate matters, Talleyrand had even offered, whether sincerely or officially was not certain, the whole of Louisiana to Livingston on April 11, the day before Monroe's arrival in Paris. He had dangled Louisiana in front of the American diplomat and then seemed to snatch it out of reach: The French minister denied that he had the proper authorization to make the offer; he said he had asked on a whim: "The idea merely struck me."[1] Desperate to salvage his two-year mission and gain some credit for any possible deal regarding the Mississippi Valley region, Livingston chose to press Talleyrand and try and get something official out of him. To that end, he sent the French diplomat a note on April 12 which practically pleaded for "Something in the form of a note or letter on your part, couched in generous terms. You could express the friendship of the First Consul for the United States, his desire to give them striking indication of it in ceding the whole of Louisiana to them. . . . We could work to mature the treaty even before the formal reception of Mr. Monroe. . . ."[2] Before the formal reception of Monroe, Livingston dearly wanted for any deal concerning the purchase of Louisiana to bear his fingerprints, not those of some recently arrived negotiator who had not struggled through the weave and dodge of French diplomacy over the previous two years. Even as he was driven to hope for a quick deal, though, he ended his letter to Talleyrand similarly to the way Talleyrand ended their talk the previous day, with a disclaimer: "Please, Sir," Livingston had written, "regard this as unofficial."[3]

Although Livingston stepped up the call for the making of a deal over Louisiana, he was still flailing in the dark. One important piece of information that neither Jefferson nor Madison had ever given Livingston had to do with money. He had never been told how much he was authorized to offer or accept for the purchase of New Orleans, West Florida, or Louisiana. He had asked Madison repeatedly, even emotionally, for a range of amounts he could offer, but to no avail. Livingston had always negotiated with the French with at least one arm tied behind his back. Now Talleyrand, even if in jest, was asking the question: What would the United States give for the whole of Louisiana?

NEW NEGOTIATORS, NEW NEGOTIATIONS

Despite Livingston's attempts, no true deal was made before Monroe arrived at Livingston's house on the Right Bank of the Seine at Rue Trudon on the evening of April 12, a Tuesday. (Today, that street no longer exists, but it was located near the new Paris opera house, the same one of "Phantom" fame.) Little official business was done at that time, and the two negotiators agreed to meet the following day to go over Monroe's instructions from Jefferson and Madison, as well as Livingston's lengthy file of letters and other communications from the past months. Still, the two men were in the same room, had been sent by the same government, and were both bound to the same cause, and events were moving quickly.

It is at this point in the historical record that the chain of events, including who was responsible for what success in the purchasing of Louisiana becomes a bit vague. As one historian has written: "Livingston's and Monroe's contemporary notes and correspondence about the Louisiana Purchase are replete with vague or inaccurate dates, loose ends, dead ends, and occasional misinformation."[4] That a purchase of Louisiana by the United States from France happened is certain, historical fact. Who did what and when over the days following April 12, however, remains a gray area. Yes, Monroe would offer his

April 30, 1803: Statesmen James Monroe (1758–1831) and Robert R. Livingston (1746–1813) are depicted here completing negotiations with Charles Maurice de Talleyrand (1754–1838) for the Louisiana Purchase.

account of the deal making years later in his memoirs. So did Barbé-Marbois. Those do not agree in the details, however. What appears clear is that both Livingston and Monroe would later try and claim as much credit for each of themselves as possible.

Nevertheless, the credit belongs to both of them. Livingston informed Monroe at their meeting on the evening of the April 12 that he had met with Talleyrand just hours earlier. The French minister had continued to be evasive, but he asked, once again, for Livingston to offer a price for Louisiana. As the conversation continued, Talleyrand eventually stated what he had claimed many times over: That "Louisiana was not theirs." Then, Livingston seemed to panic Talleyrand by responding: "If so we should negotiate no further on the subject but advise our Government to take possession." In response, the French minister "seemed alarmed."[5] Later, during his evening meeting with Monroe, Livingston stated that he had come away from his talks with Talleyrand that day "[sensing] that something bigger was going on."[6]

Then, on April 13, after Livingston and Monroe had spent a day discussing their strategy and poring over official papers, then enjoying an evening dinner with their assistants, a strange event took place. From the dinner table, Livingston looked out into his garden, only to see someone outside. Someone at the table observed: "Doesn't that look like Barbé-Marbois out there?" It was then that an excited Livingston noted: "It is. It is!"[7] Uncertain of the protocol of finding the French minister of finance in his garden after dark, Livingston sent out one of his sons-in-law to greet him. Barbé-Marbois did not explain why he was in the garden, and no one put him on the spot by asking. He was invited in to share cognac with the Americans, but said he would come back in an hour when the meal was fully completed. Return he did, while the Americans were taking their coffee. Not long after entering Livingston's house, he turned to his host and asked to meet with him in the next room, just the two of them.

Asking to speak with Livingston alone was a bit of an awkward request. Although Livingston had been the American diplomat the French had dealt with for many months, Monroe had arrived now, and he was Livingston's superior. The new American arrival, however, had not been officially recognized by the French court, so Barbé-Marbois's diplomatic etiquette was technically correct. The two men did talk for a bit, with Livingston telling the minister of finance that he had had two conversations regarding Louisiana with Talleyrand, one that very day. Barbé-Marbois did not reveal any response, but listened intently. As the two men spoke, the French official dangled the bait under Livingston's nose. We need to talk elsewhere, he said, given the house is busy with people. Should we continue our discussion, Barbé-Marbois hinted, it would "lead to something important that had been cursorily mentioned to him at St. Cloud [where he had met with Bonaparte]." Soon, he asked Livingston to come to the treasury minister's office. Livingston agreed.[8]

After Barbé-Marbois left, Livingston told Monroe of the upcoming meeting at Barbé-Marbois's. Monroe was uncertain:

> I hesitated on the idea of Livingston's going to see Marbois alone. I intimated delicately that this might be showing too much zeal—that a little reserve might have a better effect. He only talked of the government's rigorous etiquette, the impropriety of my going with him. I stopped trying to change his plan, but I reminded him that he had not even read the instructions I had brought for him. In short, I said, if you must go, go to hear and not to speak.[9]

DOWN TO BRASS TACKS

With those words from Monroe, Livingston left to rendezvous at the treasury minister's office, arriving some time before 11 p.m. He did not leave until around midnight. Barbé-Marbois opened their second round of talks for the evening by asking Livingston to repeat what he had told Talleyrand about purchasing Louisiana. Livingston did so. Then, Livingston encouraged the finance minister to get down to brass tacks. After all, should their two countries fail to come to a conclusion regarding Louisiana, it might "enable Britain to take possession" of Louisiana.[10] The two men then discussed the possibilities of war with England and the possible role that the Americans might be driven to play should the fate of Louisiana be in question. Barbé-Marbois then recounted his recent Sunday with Bonaparte and was quite frank in revealing the gist of it all. As he talked of the first consul's resolve to sell Louisiana, Barbé-Marbois then hit on the price that Bonaparte had mentioned, quoting the French leader: "Let them give you one hundred millions and pay their own claims, and take the whole country [Louisiana]."[11]

At last! An amount was on the table. Bonaparte, of course, had only mentioned 50 million francs, but Barbé-Marbois was looking for bargaining room. Livingston did not hesitate in his answer; in fact, his facial expression told the story before he said a word. He told the French official that the amount was far too high, that the U.S. government "had not the means of raising it."[12] Barbé-Marbois immediately agreed, but asked Livingston to consider it anyway and warned him that Bonaparte might withdraw the offer to sell Louisiana at any moment. Livingston also reminded his counterpart that President Jefferson was actually only interested in New Orleans and West Florida; that the government would not be prepared to pay much for the remainder of Louisiana. Should the French lower their asking price, Livingston told Barbé-Marbois, there might be grounds for a deal.

Although the deal was not struck during that late hour of the night, great strides had been made by both sides. To begin, the French were finally admitting they owned Louisiana and that they had the right to sell it. (Talleyrand, even earlier that same day, had denied his country had possession of the North American territory.) Also, France and the United States were no longer talking about "whether France might sell Louisiana or whether the United States might buy it. Livingston and Barbé-Marbois had begun to negotiate a price.

It was a part of the deal making that Barbé-Marbois wanted desperately to nail down that evening. He was, after all, under orders from Bonaparte to see to the deal as quickly as possible. When Livingston would not even hazard a guess without consulting with others, the French negotiator even gave him some help. Livingston's counterpart went so far as to suggest "that if we should name sixty million and take upon us the Americans claims to the amount of twenty more he would see how far it would be accepted."[13] Neither man could know with certainty that, although negotiations would continue over the following two weeks, that 60 million francs would, indeed, be the price the Americans would agree to pay for Louisiana. At that moment, Livingston still claimed the amount was too much.

Despite the late hour, Barbé-Marbois was prepared to finish the process then and there. He indicated as much to Livingston

JAMES MONROE
(1758–1831)

Envoy-Extraordinary

Monroe, like Jefferson, was a Virginian by heritage, born into a modest planter family in April 1758. As a young man, he attended the College of William and Mary in the commonwealth's capital at Williamsburg, where he found his classes largely boring. Fortunately for the bored Monroe, the American Revolutionary War interrupted his studies. Although only 17 years old, Monroe joined the Third Virginia Regiment and soon saw action in a small clash of arms on Manhattan Island in 1775. Perhaps his greatest day of the war was his participation in an assault against a German artillery position during the battle of Trenton on Christmas Day, 1776. That day, he suffered a wound that severed an artery in his shoulder, causing him to nearly bleed to death. For his actions at Trenton, Monroe was advanced in rank from captain to major to colonel the following year. (Washington himself would describe young Monroe in a letter "as a brave, active, and sensible officer.")* He was given a staff assignment to one of General Washington's brigade leaders, William Alexander. It was while serving Alexander that Monroe, who spoke a little French, became associated with the Marquis de Lafayette, who was an aide to Washington.

when he spoke the following, words that the American negotiator later told Monroe:

> Says he, you know the temper of a youthful conqueror—
> every thing he does is rapid as lightening[.] We have only
> to speak to him as an opportunity presents itself, perhaps in
> a crowd when he bears no contradiction. When I am alone
> with him I can speak more freely and he attends but this

Again, Monroe was faced with boredom as a staff officer, so he gave up his commission in 1778 and returned to his native Virginia where he studied law under Thomas Jefferson. It would be the beginning of their lifelong friendship. In 1782, Monroe was elected to the Virginia House of Delegates and then served in the national government as a representative to the Confederation Congress from 1783 until 1786. During these formative years for his new country, Monroe became a friend of westerners by opposing the closing of the Mississippi River to American commerce in exchange for Spanish trade concessions. He also helped draft the Northwest Ordinance which helped organize the western territories north of the Ohio River. During President Washington's administration, he was appointed as resident minister to France in 1794. After his recall two years later because of his controversial support of the French Revolution, he returned again to Virginia, where he was elected governor and served from 1799 until 1802. It was at the end of Monroe's term as governor that President Jefferson summoned his old friend for a mission to France.

*Jon Kukla, A Wilderness So Immense: The Louisiana Purchase and the Destiny of America. *New York: Knopf, 2003, p. 47.*

opportunity seldom happens and is always accidental. Try then if you can not come up to my mark. Consider the extent of the country, the exclusive navigation of the River, and the importance of having no neighbour to dispute with you, no war to dread.[14]

Napoleon Bonaparte could back out at any moment; opportunity only knocks once; the United States will have full control of the Mississippi; no other European power will dominate the lands west of the United States; you will not have to worry about going to war: Let's make the deal. Livingston stood firm, however, and did not agree prematurely. He did ask the French finance minister a probing question: If the French sold Louisiana, would France also agree never to take control of the Floridas from Spain or any other future power? Surprisingly, Barbé-Marbois said his country would agree to that stipulation. Then, Livingston probed his French friend regarding Talleyrand. In so many words, the American wanted to know if the foreign minister had the authority to deal over Louisiana or if it might be someone else, such as Barbé-Marbois. The French finance minister made it clear that, when it came to negotiating over the Mississippi Valley, he spoke with the authority of the first consul.

There was nothing left to talk about. Livingston took his leave of the French finance minister and told him he would update Monroe on everything they had discussed at that late hour. Livingston did not wait until morning to relay information regarding his discussion with Barbé-Marbois to someone, however. At three that morning, he was still up, writing a letter to Secretary of State James Madison. "Thus, Sir, you see a negotiation is fairly opened," Livingston wrote to Madison. "We shall do all we can to cheapen the purchase but my present sentiment is that we shall buy."[15] By the time Livingston finally crawled wearily off to bed, the day had been exceptionally long and wonderfully productive.

This is a view of Paris as it looked in the early nineteenth century, as seen from the Pont Royal, one of the many bridges that span the River Seine. The Louvre is the large building on the right.

DIFFICULTIES AHEAD

The following day, April 14, a Thursday, with Livingston having updated Monroe on the night's progress, the two Americans went to the offices of Foreign Minister Talleyrand, who accepted Monroe's credentials and recognized him as speaking for the United States. Talleyrand reported that Bonaparte was pleased with the discussions so far. He also promised to present Monroe to the first consul as soon as possible. Monroe was leery of a delay. Typically, ministers such as himself were presented to Bonaparte during public audiences, and the next one was scheduled for more than two weeks later, on May 1, at the Louvre. But Talleyrand assured them that the discussions over Louisiana could continue regardless of whether Monroe had been presented formally to the first consul. He was right. What was at stake was too important for

Bonaparte to stand on ceremony or protocol and slow down the negotiations.

There was a problem with continuing the discussions over Louisiana, however—an obstacle that was complicating matters. Under the Treaty of San Ildefonso, Spain had agreed to return Louisiana to the French, but with the understanding that the French would not rid themselves of the property except by handing it back to the Spanish. Thus, any discussion between France and the United States was a violation of that treaty. Nevertheless, both sides in these negotiations appeared ready to swing wide of that stipulation. No one in Spain could easily stand in Bonaparte's way of making a transfer to the United States. President Jefferson might have a problem among opposition party leaders in the Senate, however. Under the Constitution, the Senate must ratify all treaties.

The following day, April 15, both Livingston and Monroe sat down together opposite Barbé-Marbois. There was so much both sides had already agreed upon, even if just by way of tacit understanding. Nevertheless, all three were not yet on the same page. That day, Monroe wrote his own letter to Madison in which he made it clear he was not completely pleased with Livingston's actions since the new minister had arrived in Paris just days earlier. Monroe had a friend in Fulwar Skipwith, who was then the American commercial agent in Paris. They had worked together during the 1790s when Monroe had served as minister to France. Skipwith had informed Monroe that Livingston was working hard "to turn the occurrences in America and even my mission to his account."[16] Translation: Livingston was trying to position himself to take the credit when a deal was finally made. Even though the two Americans were not seeing eye to eye and were actually acting as if they were competing with one another, the bargaining over Louisiana continued.

Deal of the Century

They continued to meet with Barbé-Marbois for a full week, mostly haggling over the price of the property. Meanwhile, the whole process faced the possibility of being completely derailed. There was serious French opposition, including Admiral Decrès and Bonaparte's own brothers, Lucien and Joseph. Such opposition sometimes worked to the Americans' advantage. When talks hit a snag or stalled, Livingston and Monroe tried to get Barbé-Marbois to lower his asking price for the property. (Quietly, secretly, the two American diplomats had agreed that they would pay as much as 50 million francs but publicly would only agree to pay 40 million.) Only when the finance minister indicated that he might be replaced by Talleyrand if a deal was not soon made, did Monroe and Livingston raise their accepted price tag to 50 million francs.

THE DIPLOMATIC DANCE CONTINUES

Diplomacy, with all its deceptions, feints, and threats, continued. Once the Americans agreed to 50 million francs, Barbé-Marbois indicated that Bonaparte might not only reject the figure, but might be so offended that he would pull Louisiana off the market. He was bluffing, of course, for 50 million had been Bonaparte's asking price all along. Then, negotiations seemed to stop once again as both sides assessed their positions. As Livingston would write, "We were all resting on our oars."[1] The strain of the negotiations soon manifested itself as Monroe developed back trouble, which put him in bed. On Thursday, April 27, Barbé-Marbois, who was becoming frustrated and impatient, visited Monroe, with Livingston present, and handed the Americans two written proposals, with Monroe propped up as comfortably as possible on a sofa. Both proposals were surprise lightning bolts. The first proposal was that the Americans, if purchasing Louisiana, would have to offer France the modern-day equivalent of most-favored-nation status concerning trade and commerce in New Orleans. Second, the price was going back up to 100 million francs, the amount Barbé-Marbois had insisted upon when he first sat down with Livingston on the night of April 13, 10 days ago.

The Americans had worked too hard to purchase Louisiana to give up any progress they had made to date, however. Monroe and Livingston did not agree, and Barbé-Marbois himself did not even agree, dismissing the French government's expectations as "hard and unreasonable."[2] Then, Barbé-Marbois handed them a copy of a treaty, written in his own hand, that provided "France and Spain limited commercial privileges in New Orleans and arranged for settling U.S. claims."[3] He then said it was an agreement that Bonaparte might agree to. The only thing missing was the amount the Americans were willing to pay. The two Americans left, went back to their apartments, and took their pens to the treaty, with both diplomats making alterations in the section Barbé-Marbois had worded regarding U.S. claims. An agreement had not yet, even after two weeks of negotiations, been made, but the end was near.

The following day, April 28, Thursday, Livingston wrote up a new draft, using Barbé-Marbois's as his template. He and Monroe then met with Barbé-Marbois the next day. The American proposal was 50 million francs for Louisiana and 20 million that would be used to repay American citizens who had made claims against the French government. Barbé-Marbois stood firm, telling his counterparts that anything less than 80 million francs total would not be acceptable. Then, suddenly, Livingston and Monroe agreed to the 80 million. They even outlined a proposal to pay for the Louisiana Purchase by borrowing through European banks. They agreed to a 12-year most-favored-nation trading status for French merchants doing business in the port of New Orleans. Barbé-Marbois then brought up another point that appeared quite important to him. He wanted to make certain that those living in Louisiana, especially French peoples, would be treated fairly, not removed out, and that their rights would be protected. Livingston and Monroe saw no reason to balk and, in the final version of the treaty, those assurances were included in Article III:

> The inhabitants of the ceded territory shall be incorporated in the Union of the United States and admitted as soon as possible according to the principles of the federal Constitution to the enjoyment of all these rights, advantages and immunities of citizens of the United States, and in the mean time they shall be maintained and protected in the free enjoyment of their liberty, property and the Religion which they profess.[4]

AT LAST, A DEAL

The long-awaited deal of the new nineteenth century was completed. Eighty million francs was the final price, equal to approximately $15 million dollars. Of that figure, the French government would receive 60 million francs ($11,250,000) and the remaining 20 million ($3,750,000) would pay off claims against France made by mostly American merchants and shippers who had been victimized by French privateers during the undeclared naval war of the late 1790s. On April 29, 1803, then, all aspects of the treaty and its wording were concluded. The following day, they met again, looked the document over one more time and initialed the treaty.

Every day inched the formalities along. On May 1, the two Americans had dinner with Bonaparte and, that evening, an official reception was held at the Louvre in honor of the agreement. Then, the three negotiators met on May 2 in Barbé-Marbois's office, and the treaty was signed. They had come to know one another well during the previous weeks of hard negotiating, and the Frenchman and the two Americans saw themselves as engaged in a momentous event. As they shook hands with one another, Livingston spoke:

> We have lived long, but this is the noblest work of our whole lives. The treaty which we have just signed has not been obtained by art or dictated by force. . . . It will change vast solitudes into flourishing districts. From this day the United States take their place among the powers of the first rank.[5]

The first consul of France was also pleased with the conclusion of the deal over Louisiana. "The negotiations leave me nothing to wish," he stated to Barbé-Marbois.[6] He, too, saw the Louisiana Purchase as momentous for the young United States. Noting to his finance minister: "This accession of territory strengthens for ever the power of the United States."[7]

PREPARING FOR WAR

Immediately, Bonaparte ushered a secretary into his office and gave him an order to begin spending the vast amount of money that would be forthcoming to the French treasury on five canals for the purpose of benefiting domestic business and trade. The French leader was only providing headlines for the newspapers,

This is a photograph of the Louisiana Purchase Treaty, signed April 30, 1803, with a map of New Orleans in the background.

however. He had no intention of spending the money on French canals or on anything else to improve the infrastructure of his country. Instead, he spent all of it preparing his military for an invasion of Great Britain, his longstanding enemy. Within two weeks of the conclusion of the Louisiana Purchase, France and England were at war—again.

There would be war, but the French invasion of Great Britain that Napoleon Bonaparte had dreamed of for so long never occurred. Despite doubts and criticisms from French admirals, the first consul began spending America's Louisiana Purchase money in stacks, amassing a force of 200,000—his "Army of England"—even as French engineers and boatman cobbled together 2,000 specially designed flatboats to carry his army across the English Channel. His admirals insisted the flatboats were not practical and that these "flat-bottomed landing craft would be smashed to driftwood by the royal navy if British men-of-war caught them on the open sea."[8]

PREMATURE PLANS FOR AN AMERICAN EXPEDITION

Even before the United States had negotiated the vast region of Louisiana as its own, President Thomas Jefferson was making plans for his fellow Americans to explore it. In time, these plans would become the famous Lewis and Clark Expedition. The president had first thought of such an undertaking about the time the United States had achieved its independence, in 1783. On January 18, 1803, Jefferson asked Congress for authorization and an appropriation of $2500 to send a military expedition to explore the Missouri River, to find its source in the Rocky Mountains, then to follow the western-flowing streams to the Pacific.

Jefferson gave two purposes for the proposed mission: to prepare the way for the expansion of the American fur trade to the tribes throughout the area to be explored; and to advance geographical knowledge of the continent. (At the time, the region was not yet owned by the United States, because the Louisiana Purchase was not yet signed.)

While the proposal was before Congress, events lined up in Jefferson's favor. By April 1803, the French had negotiated for the sale of the vast Louisiana Territory to the Americans. With that purchase, there were no realistic impediments to Congress authorizing such an expedition into the West.

Even though the treaty transferring ownership of Louisiana from France to the United States was agreed upon in April, the treaty was not ratified until October 1803. This did not stop the progress on the proposed expedition. The commanders of the expedition included Captain Meriwether Lewis, Jefferson's private secretary, and an old

Aware of Napoleon's obvious preparations, the British were in a near panic. The government called for 300,000 volunteers to meet the possible French invasion force, even though they

army friend of his, William Clark. Through the summer of 1803, as word of the new purchase agreement filtered back to the United States from France, Captain Lewis was busy purchasing supplies and equipment for the expedition and both leaders were working hard putting their group of explorers together.

By the fall of 1803, Lewis, Clark, and most of the young men who would accompany them on the trail west across the upper reaches of Louisiana were already in St. Louis, which was still under the control of Spanish officials. That fall, the party was prepared to head up the Missouri, but the Spanish in St. Louis would not allow them to enter Spanish territory. Those officials had not yet heard that the Louisiana Purchase Treaty had been ratified by the U.S. Senate. This turn of events caused the expedition to remain on the Illinois side of the Mississippi River through the winter of 1803–1804. By then, all the documents of transfer of the territory had been signed, all the legal obstacles removed, and the official handover of the territory had taken place in New Orleans. Thus, although the plans for the Lewis and Clark Expedition had begun before the Americans had actually bought the vast interior region of Louisiana, it was clearly U.S. property by the time the men in the expedition began their trek up the mighty Missouri River toward the unknown west of Louisiana. In fact, in April 1804, just weeks after the movement of Lewis and Clark's Corps of Discovery up the Missouri River, Americans back East were celebrating the one-year anniversary of the purchase of Louisiana and the deal that Livingston, Monroe, and Barbé-Marbois had hammered out in 1803.

had no way of arming two out of every three of them. Desperately, British officials even secretly dispatched a team of assassins, which included 60 Frenchmen who absolutely despised Bonaparte, to France to murder the French leader. Among their number was a former French general.

When the plot was uncovered by Bonaparte's secret police, the first consul called off the invasion until his would-be killers were ferreted out. When the assassins were finally rounded up, they identified Louis-Antoine-Henri de Bourbon-Condé, duc d'Enghien, an exiled French aristocrat and relative of Louis XVI as their co-conspirator. Bonaparte had him seized and brought to him. The French leader carried out Enghien's punishment himself, shooting the conspirator at sunrise.

By the spring of 1805, Napoleonic armies were on the march to the East, engaging the armies of Russia and Austria with smashing success. Bonaparte's plans for an invasion of England, however, were collapsing. His flatboats, indeed, were not seaworthy. He had launched several dozen of his boats, loaded with hundreds of men and their equipment during heavy weather, and his flatboats had floundered, drowning more than 500 of Bonaparte's troops. Only then did he finally give up his dream of a French flotilla landing on the shores of England.

As for the English response to the Louisiana Purchase, the British government had no significant problems with the transfer of Louisiana to the United States (better in the hands of the Americans than the French, they thought). The sale also provided business for one of England's largest banking houses, Baring Brothers. Along with a Dutch banking firm, Amsterdam's Hope and Company, these two lending institutions provided most of the monies. This put the funds in Bonaparte's hands quickly, making him, as well as the bankers themselves, happy. Their commission for lending the funds for the land transfer would amount to nearly $3 million.

Although there were some questions about the exact boundaries of the newly purchased territory (the earlier Treaty of San

Ildefonso between the Spanish and French had not nailed down clear boundaries, either), the territory was estimated to include 875,000 square miles (2,266,239 square kilometers). (When the exact boundaries were finally drawn up in 1819, the size of the Louisiana Purchase Territory was determined to be 529,402,880 acres.) Quick math tells how great a bargain the Americans had made for the vast, uncharted territory—just over three cents an acre. There would be other costs beyond the original 60 million francs that was actually the purchase price (minus the 20 million in indemnities), however. Because the purchase was financed over a 20-year term, the amount ultimately paid for Louisiana, by 1823, was almost twice 60 million francs. By the time everything was included and accounted for in the costs of the transfer of Louisiana on paper to the Americans, the actual price tag was closer to $27 million.

SELLING LOUISIANA TO THE NATION

By May 13, Livingston and Monroe sent a lengthy letter to Secretary of State Madison, explaining what they had accomplished and why they had agreed to every aspect of the deal. Back in the United States, word eventually arrived of the purchase of Louisiana. Historians believe that the news reached President Jefferson in the Executive Mansion on July 3, with the next day being Independence Day. As far as the public was concerned, they heard, in dribs and drabs, over the following weeks and even months. Even before the president received definitive word on the purchase, it was in some newspapers. The Boston *Independent Chronicle* and the *New York Evening Post* both ran the story on Thursday, June 30. The Boston paper referred to the purchase as the result of "wise, seasonable and political negociation"[9] and used the headline "LOUISIANA CEDED TO THE UNITED STATES!" The *New York Morning Chronicle*, another of New York City's important newspapers, however, did not report on the purchase until July 21.

The details of the Louisiana Purchase were nothing short of inspiring to many Americans. John Quincy Adams, son of second president John Adams, judged the purchase as "next in historical importance to the *Declaration of Independence* and the adoption of the *Constitution*. It was unparalleled in diplomacy because it cost almost nothing."[10] From one part of the country to the next, excitement was the watchword. No section of the country received the news of the Louisiana Purchase with more enthusiasm than the West, however. For many of those American pioneers, frontiersmen, and other western residents who had become dependent on the Mississippi River and New Orleans for their livelihood, they naturally "reacted like lottery winners who find their good fortune unbelievable."[11] Americans from Ohio to Kentucky to Tennessee were ecstatic about the security their lives had gained by the purchase. No longer could a foreign power hold the fate of America's trans-Appalachian West in its hands. New Orleans was now an American port.

There were those Americans who did not seem prepared to rally excitedly behind the greatest land purchase in U.S. history. Most of them belonged to the opposition party to Jefferson's Republicans. The Federalists, in Congress and otherwise, "thought up snide, half-humorous ways to attack the bargain purchase of nearly half a continent, calling it an extravagance."[12] The Dutch had purchased Manhattan Island from the Indians for $24, they quipped. Perhaps $15 million was too much for land that was largely nothing more than wilderness. One Federalist complained: "We are to give money of which we have too little for land of which we already have too much."[13] One Federalist leader did not harangue about the treaty. Alexander Hamilton of New York believed the purchase was vital to the United States. The spread of the nation further West would eventually help the country become a world power. A longstanding political enemy of Thomas Jefferson's, Hamilton did not give the president any credit for the deal. Instead, he explained it as "the kind interpositions of an over-ruling Providence."[14] Ultimately, even Federalist senators could not ignore the landslide of enthusiasm that was sweeping the country over the transfer of Louisiana from French control to American ownership.

Ironically, one uncertain American was Thomas Jefferson himself. Although he had supported the purchase of Louisiana in theory, once the deal was struck, he had concerns about its legality. Jefferson was a strict-constructionist regarding the U.S. Constitution, meaning he interpreted the document and the powers it bestowed on the three branches of government by a narrow criteria. If a power was not expressly mentioned, it probably did not exist. This position coincided with his view that the states of the Union held broad powers and rights, while the federal government should hold only limited power. The federal government was now poised to purchase land without the direct consent of the states. In addition, he was uncertain the Constitution made provision for the purchase of property from a foreign government. Such hand-wringing seems, to the modern observer, to have occurred to Jefferson a bit late in the game.

On July 16, he called a meeting of his Cabinet and told his advisers that he believed the Constitution might need to be amended to allow the annexation of Louisiana. He actually wrote a draft of such an amendment. Jefferson soon realized, however, that his Cabinet was not really concerned about the annexation and was not interested in a new amendment to the Constitution. They also reminded him that the deadline for ratification of the treaty was set for October 30, 1803, only three months away. There was no way for a new amendment to work its way through Congress and face ratification by the states within that timeframe. Congress was not even scheduled to come back into session again until November!

Jefferson soon decided to call a special session of Congress for October 17, to provide time for the Senate to approve the treaty and for the House of Representatives to approve the monies for the purchase. Then, he ordered the governor of the Mississippi Territory, William C. C. Claiborne, and General James Wilkinson, the commander of the U.S. Army, to take immediate steps to occupy the city of New Orleans. Jefferson would soon drop his doubts when he received new word from Livingston: Bonaparte appeared to be backing out of the deal. In Livingston's words, the French leader "appears to wish the thing undone."[15] As for this change of heart on the part of Bonaparte, Livingston blamed Talleyrand. There were other reasons, of course, including Spain's reaction to the deal. The Spanish were furious to learn of the purchase, and immediately accused Bonaparte of violating the Treaty of San Ildefonso by having handed off Louisiana to a third party. When Jefferson learned about Spain's anger, he became concerned that the Spanish might not surrender control of New Orleans. It is at this point—by now it was the first week of October—that the strict constructionist Jefferson, the president who was so concerned over whether the Louisiana Purchase was legal or not, met with his Cabinet and asked if they would support the takeover of New Orleans by military force if the Spanish did not cooperate in giving up New Orleans. Each Cabinet member voted yes.

Military action proved unnecessary, though. Jefferson addressed Congress on October 17 and presented the members with the Louisiana Purchase Treaty. Then, with almost no debate, the Senate voted, and the treaty was ratified by a tally of 24 to 7. Every Republican, plus a Federalist senator from New Jersey, William Plume, voted for the treaty. The vote in the House to fund the purchase was never in question, since Republican representatives outnumbered Federalists by three to one. The vote was overwhelmingly in favor: 90 to 25. Of the 25 Federalists who rejected the funding, 17 came from New England.

A NEW AMERICAN TERRITORY

As the Louisiana Purchase became more of a true reality during the summer and fall of 1803, earlier events related to Louisiana were coming to a tragic close. Even though Bonaparte had finally given up on his dream of a French empire in Louisiana, he had not completely abandoned the French struggle to gain control of Santo Domingo. The fight had continued and, by that summer, General Rochambeau had seemed to gain the upper hand on the island. Once Bonaparte began implementing his plans for war with Great Britain, however, the British West Indies fleet set a course for Santo Domingo, where they bombarded French positions and ran guns to the black rebels, who had never surrendered. By August, ironically, Rochambeau was writing to President Jefferson to send him money to help him continue his fight. No American money was sent, though, and the French subsequently took refuge in four of the island's ports, where they awaited their destructive end. With his army starving to death, Rochambeau finally signed an armistice with the island's rebels in November. This was followed by his surrender to British naval forces. At last, the French campaign to stamp out black rebellion on Santo Domingo had reached its bitter conclusion.

Over the following months, the transfer of Louisiana to the United States became a physical reality as well as a paper agreement. In New Orleans, the French prefect, Pierre Clement de Laussat, informed the residents that they would soon become American citizens. Laussat expressed no bitterness or resentment, but told the people that the purchase symbolized a "pledge of friendship" between France and the United States. Then, Laussat sent a message to American officials in the Mississippi river town of Natchez that he was prepared to hand off Louisiana to them. General Wilkinson had already visited New Orleans, where he found only 300 ill-prepared Spanish soldiers comprising the local garrison. There had been a call for 6,000 militia to stand by, in case the port city needed to be taken by the Americans by force. Wilkinson had let Governor Claiborne know that the reinforcements would not be needed, however—the city could be taken by, in Wilkinson's words, 500 mounted Tennesseeans.

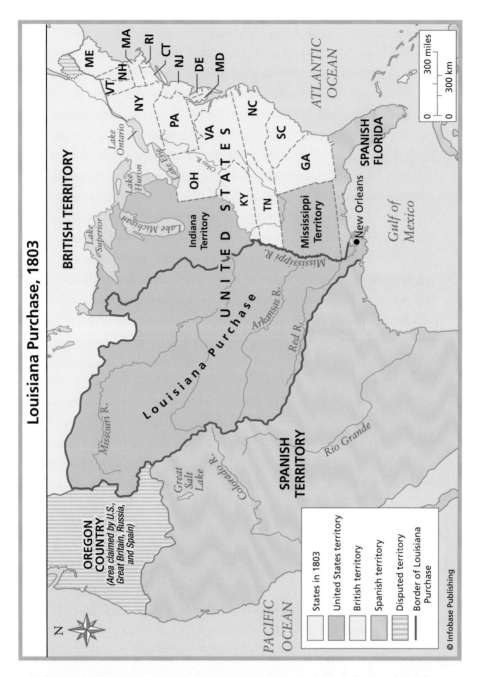

Louisiana Purchase, 1803

BRITISH TERRITORY

Lake Superior

Lake Michigan

Lake Huron

Lake Ontario

Lake Erie

Ohio R.

ME

VT

NH

MA

RI

CT

NY

NJ

PA

DE

MD

OH

VA

NC

KY

TN

SC

GA

UNITED STATES

Indiana Territory

Mississippi Territory

New Orleans

SPANISH FLORIDA

ATLANTIC OCEAN

Gulf of Mexico

Mississippi R.

Louisiana Purchase

Arkansas R.

Red R.

Missouri R.

SPANISH TERRITORY

Rio Grande

Great Salt Lake

Colorado R.

OREGON COUNTRY
(Area claimed by U.S., Great Britain, Russia, and Spain)

PACIFIC OCEAN

N

300 miles

300 km

0

0

States in 1803

United States territory

British territory

Spanish territory

Disputed territory

Border of Louisiana Purchase

© Infobase Publishing

This map shows the area of land that was included in the Louisiana Purchase.

In the end, such military force was not necessary. When the Americans arrived, led by Governor Claiborne and General Wilkinson, they were unopposed and even welcomed. On December 20, an official ceremony was held along the banks of the Mississippi at the Place d'Armes. Laussat was present, and so were Claiborne and Wilkinson. They, and a large crowd, one that included Spanish, French, and American observers, "watched while the French tricolor was lowered and the American stars and stripes ascended the flagpole."[16] As Laussat wept, the Americans present on the scene, although small in number, cheered when their flag reached the top of the pole. The Louisiana Purchase, an agreement long sought after by a nation determined to move further and further West, toward a destiny of which many were certain, even if its details were unclear, was finally reality.

CHRONOLOGY

1682 French explorer Robert Cavelier, Sieur de La Salle, reaches the mouth of the Mississippi River after floating down the river from the north; he will name the territory watered by the Mississippi River *Louisiana*.

1699 The LeMoyne brothers (Pierre, d'Iberville, and Jean-Baptiste, d'Bienville) establish the colony of Louisiana for France; their initial settlement site was located at modern-day Biloxi, Mississippi.

TIMELINE

1682
French explorer Robert Cavelier, Sieur de La Salle, reaches the mouth of the Mississippi River. He will name the territory watered by the Mississippi River *Louisiana*.

1763
France is forced to cede the portion of Louisiana east of the Mississippi River to the British.

1795
Pinckney's Treaty (also known as the Treaty of San Lorenzo) is completed and the United States is guaranteed the "right of deposit" in New Orleans for the next three years.

1682 ——————————————— **1795**

1718
New Orleans is founded by the French.

1762
The Treaty of Fontainebleau is made between the Spanish and the French.

1791
A massive slave revolt begins in the French Caribbean island colony of Santo Domingo.

1718   New Orleans is founded by the French; in time, it will become the capital of the Louisiana colony.

1762   The Treaty of Fontainebleau is made between the Spanish and the French; the treaty calls for the transfer of the western portion of the Louisiana Territory to the Spanish.

1763   Under the Treaty of Paris ending the Seven Years' War (known as the French and Indian War in America), France is forced to cede the portion of Louisiana east of the Mississippi River to the British.

1768   French Louisiana planters rise up against the first appointed Spanish official and expel him.

October 1, 1800
Second Treaty of San Ildefonso is negotiated between France and Spain. The treaty, kept secret, included Spain's agreement to retrocede the Louisiana Territory to France.

April 10, 1803
Napoleon Bonaparte meets with Barbé-Marbois and Decrès to discuss the sale of Louisiana to the Americans
April 30, 1803
The Louisiana Purchase is concluded with Bonaparte agreeing to sell all of Louisiana and the city of New Orleans to the Americans.

1800   1803

October 16, 1802
The Spanish intendant (governor) of Louisiana suspends the "right of deposit" for Americans using the port of New Orleans.

November 1803
The Senate ratifies the Louisiana Purchase Treaty.
December 20, 1803
The French officially hand off Louisiana to the Americans during a formal ceremony in New Orleans.

1789   The French Revolution begins.

1791   A massive slave revolt begins in the French Caribbean island colony of Santo Domingo.

1795   Pinckney's Treaty (also known as the Treaty of San Lorenzo) is completed between the United States and Spain; both nations agree on the northern border of Florida, and the United States is guaranteed the "right of deposit" in New Orleans for the next three years.

1798–1800   The United States and France engage in an undeclared naval war known as the Quasi-War.

1799   Napoleon Bonaparte overthrows the existing French government, the Directory, and declares himself as the First Consul.

1800   **October 1** Second Treaty of San Ildefonso is negotiated between France and Spain; the treaty, kept secret, included Spain's agreement to retrocede the Louisiana Territory to France once certain stipulations were met.

1801   **March 21** The Convention of Aranjuez seals the deal between the French and Spanish over the retrocession of Louisiana to France.

1802   **April** President Jefferson writes a letter to Robert Livingston, American resident at the court of Napoleon Bonaparte, explaining the importance of New Orleans to western American trade and commerce.

        May Napoleon Bonaparte declares himself first consul for life.

        October 16 The Spanish intendant (governor) of Louisiana suspends the "right of deposit" for Americans using the port of New Orleans.

1803 **January** Jefferson encourages the U.S. Senate to confirm the appointment of Robert Livingston and James Monroe to negotiate with the French over the purchase of New Orleans and West Florida.

April 10 Napoleon Bonaparte meets with Barbé-Marbois and Decrès to discuss the sale of Louisiana to the Americans.

April 11 Bonaparte tells Barbé-Marbois to negotiate over Louisiana; that same day, Talleyrand makes an unofficial "offer" to sell Louisiana to Livingston.

April 12 James Monroe arrives in Paris and meets with his diplomatic counterpart, Robert Livingston.

April 30 The Louisiana Purchase is concluded with Napoleon Bonaparte agreeing to sell all of Louisiana, including the city of New Orleans, to the Americans.

May 2 The most important Louisiana Purchase Treaty document is signed in Paris.

October 17 President Jefferson addresses Congress and encourages the ratification of the Louisiana Purchase Treaty.

October The Senate ratifies the Louisiana Purchase Treaty.

December 20 The French officially hand off Louisiana to the Americans during a formal ceremony in New Orleans.

Notes

CHAPTER 2

1. Quoted in Peter J. Kastor, *The Great Acquisition: An Introduction to the Louisiana Purchase.* Great Falls, Mont.: Lewis and Clark Interpretative Association, 2003, p. 20.
2. Quoted in Norbury L. Wayman, *Life on the River.* New York: Bonanza Books, 1971, pp. 1–2.
3. Quoted in Kastor, p. 22.
4. Ibid., p. 24.

CHAPTER 3

1. Quoted in Kastor, p. 25.
2. Ibid., p. 26.
3. Quoted in Thomas Jefferson, "Notes on the State of Virginia," in *The Portable Thomas Jefferson*, ed. Merrill D. Peterson. New York: Penguin Books, 1975, p. 35.
4. Quoted in Kastor, p. 30.
5. Ibid., p. 34.
6. Ibid., p. 37.
7. Quoted in Charles A. Cerami, *Jefferson's Great Gamble: The Remarkable Story of Jefferson, Napoleon and the Men Behind the Louisiana Purchase.* Naperville, Ill.: Sourcebooks, 2003, p. 38.

CHAPTER 4

1. Quoted in Thomas Fleming, *The Louisiana Purchase.* Hoboken, N.J.: John Wiley & Sons, 2003, p. 5.
2. Ibid.
3. Ibid., p. 6.
4. Ibid.
5. Ibid.
6. Ibid.
7. Quoted in Jon Kukla, *A Wilderness So Immense: The Louisiana Purchase and the Destiny of America.* New York: Alfred A. Knopf, 2003, p. 236.
8. Quoted in Fleming, p. 22.
9. Quoted in Kukla, p. 225.
10. Quoted in Fleming, p. 22.
11. Ibid.
12. Quoted in Kukla, p. 238.
13. Ibid.
14. Quoted in Fleming, p. 23.
15. Ibid., p. 24.
16. Ibid.

CHAPTER 5

1. Quoted in Cerami, p. 45.
2. Ibid., p. 46.
3. Quoted in Junius P. Rodriguez, ed. *The Louisiana Purchase: A Historical and Geographical Encyclopedia.* Santa Barbara, Calif.: ABC-CLIO, 2002, p. 205.
4. Quoted in Cerami, p. 50.
5. Ibid.
6. Quoted in Kukla, p. 218.
7. Quoted in Fleming, p. 28.
8. Ibid., p. 29.
9. Ibid., p. 31.
10. Ibid.
11. Quoted in Kukla, p. 222.
12. Ibid., p. 223.

CHAPTER 6

1. Quoted in Kukla, p. 225.
2. Ibid.

3. Quoted in Fleming, p. 34.
4. Ibid., p. 35.
5. Ibid.
6. Quoted in Cerami, p. 57.
7. Ibid.
8. Quoted in Kukla, p. 230.
9. Ibid.
10. Quoted in Fleming, pp. 37–38.
11. Quoted in Kukla, p. 232.
12. Ibid.
13. Ibid., p. 245.
14. Quoted in Fleming, p. 42.
15. Quoted in Kukla, p. 245.
16. Ibid.
17. Ibid., p. 246.
18. Ibid., p. 245.
19. Ibid., p. 247.
20. Ibid.
21. Ibid., p. 248.
22. Ibid.
23. Ibid., p. 249.
24. Ibid.
25. Ibid.
26. Ibid., p. 256.
27. Ibid.
28. Ibid.
29. Ibid.

CHAPTER 7
1. Ibid., p. 256.
2. Ibid.
3. Ibid.
4. Ibid., p. 257.
5. Ibid.
6. Ibid.
7. Ibid. and Kastor, p. 56.
8. Quoted in Kukla, p. 257.
9. Ibid.
10. Ibid., p. 261.
11. Ibid., pp. 262–263.

12. Ibid., p. 262.
13. Ibid., p. 263.
14. Ibid.
15. Ibid., p. 265.

CHAPTER 8
1. Quoted in Cerami, p. 170.
2. Ibid., p. 171.
3. Ibid.
4. Quoted in Kukla, p. 271.
5. Ibid., p. 272.
6. Ibid.
7. Quoted in Cerami, p. 175.
8. Quoted in Kukla, p. 273.
9. Quoted in Cerami, p. 178.
10. Quoted in Kukla, p. 274.
11. Ibid., p. 275.
12. Ibid.
13. Ibid., p. 276.
14. Ibid.
15. Ibid., p. 277.
16. Quoted in Fleming, p. 118.

CHAPTER 9
1. Quoted in Cerami, p. 179.
2. Quoted in Kukla, p. 279.
3. Quoted in Fleming, p. 124.
4. Quoted in Kukla, p. 280.
5. Ibid., p. 281.
6. Quoted in Fleming, p. 129.
7. Quoted in Kukla, p. 281.
8. Quoted in Fleming, p. 167.
9. Quoted in Kukla, p. 284.
10. Quoted in Cerami, p. 205.
11. Ibid., p. 209.
12. Ibid., p. 210.
13. Quoted in Fleming, p. 135.
14. Ibid., p. 136.
15. Ibid., p. 141.
16. Ibid., p. 154.

BIBLIOGRAPHY

Cerami, Charles A. *Jefferson's Great Gamble: The Remarkable Story of Jefferson, Napoleon and the Men Behind the Louisiana Purchase.* Naperville, Ill.: Sourcebooks, 2003.

Fleming, Thomas. *The Louisiana Purchase.* Hoboken, N.J.: John Wiley & Sons, 2003.

Jefferson, Thomas. "Notes on the State of Virginia," in *The Portable Thomas Jefferson.* Edited by Merrill D. Peterson. New York: Penguin Books, 1975.

Kastor, Peter J. *The Great Acquisition: An Introduction to the Louisiana Purchase.* Great Falls, Mont.: Lewis and Clark Interpretative Association, 2003.

Kennedy, Roger G. *Mr. Jefferson's Lost Cause: Land, Farmers, Slavery, and the Louisiana Purchase.* New York: Oxford University Press, 2003.

Kukla, Jon. *A Wilderness So Immense: The Louisiana Purchase and the Destiny of America.* New York: Alfred A. Knopf, 2003.

McCarthy, Ann. *The Mississippi River.* New York: Crescent Books, 1984.

Rodriguez, Junius P., ed. *The Louisiana Purchase: A Historical and Geographical Encyclopedia.* Santa Barbara, Calif.: ABC-CLIO, 2002.

Wayman, Norbury L. *Life on the River.* New York: Bonanza Books, 1971.

FURTHER READING

Burgan, Michael. *The Louisiana Purchase.* Minneapolis, Minn.: Compass Point Books, 2002.

Phelan, Mary Kay. *Story of the Louisiana Purchase.* New York: HarperCollins Children's Books, 1979.

Pierce, Alan. *Louisiana Purchase.* Edina, Minn.: ABDO, 2004.

Roop, Peter, and Connie Roop. *The Louisiana Purchase.* New York: Simon & Schuster Children's Publishing, 2004.

Sakurai, Gail. *Louisiana Purchase.* New York: Scholastic Library, 1998.

Sanna, Ellyn. *Thomas Jefferson's America: The Louisiana Purchase (1800–1811).* Broomall, Pa.: Mason Crest, 2004.

Schlaepfer, Gloria G. *The Louisiana Purchase.* New York: Scholastic Library, 2005.

Thompson, Linda. *Louisiana Purchase.* Vero Beach, Fl.: Rourke, 2005.

Worth, Richard. *National Geographic Voices from Colonial America.* Washington, D.C.: National Geographic Society, 2005.

Zurn, Jon. *Louisiana Purchase.* Edina, Minn.: ABDO, 2007.

WEB SITES

"The Cabildo: The Louisiana Purchase," Louisiana State Museum
http://lsm.crt.state.la.us/cabildo/cab4.htm

"Louisiana Purchase," Gateway New Orleans
http://gatewayno.com/history/LaPurchase.html

"The Louisiana Purchase," Kidport Reference Library

http://www.kidport.com/RefLib/UsaHistory/LouisianaPurchase/
    LouisianaPurc.htm

"Louisiana Purchase Bicentennial," Louisiana Purchase 2003

http://www.louisianapurchase2003.com/

"Louisiana Purchase Historical Overview," Louisiana Purchase 2003

http://www.louisianapurchase2003.com/history/overview/
    index.htm

"Louisiana Purchase State Park," Arkansas State Parks

http://www.arkansasstateparks.com/louisianapurchase/

"Louisiana Purchase Treaty, 1803," American Originals: National Archives and Records Administration

http://www.archives.gov/exhibits/american_originals_iv/
    sections/louisiana_purchase_treaty.html.

Photo Credits

PAGE

3: AP Images

6: MPI/Getty Images

9: Library of Congress, cph 3b27098.

18: Bildarchiv Preussischer Kulturbesitz/Art Resource, NY

21: The New York Public Library / Art Resource, NY

28: AP Images

30: AP Images

39: Erich Lessing/Art Resource, NY

41: Library of Congress, pga 02908

46: National Portrait Gallery, Smithsonian Institution/ Art Resource, NY

54: Library of Congress, cph 3b18334

57: Time & Life Pictures/Getty Images

72: The Granger Collection, New York

77: Scala/Art Resource, NY

87: © Bettmann/Corbis

93: Library of Congress, cph 3c04958

98: Getty Images

105: French School, Getty Images

111: Erich Lessing/Art Resource, NY

120: © Infobase Publishing

INDEX

ABOUT THE AUTHOR

TIM MCNEESE is associate professor of history at York College in York, Nebraska, where he is in his sixteenth year of college instruction. Professor McNeese earned an associate of arts degree from York College, a bachelor of arts in history and political science from Harding University, and a master of arts in history from Missouri State University. A prolific author of books for elementary-, middle-, and high-school, as well as college readers, McNeese has published more than 90 books and educational materials over the past 20 years, on everything from the founding of Jamestown to Spanish painters. His writing has earned him a citation in the library reference work, *Contemporary Authors.* In 2006, Tim appeared on the History Channel program *Risk Takers, History Makers: John Wesley Powell and the Grand Canyon.* He was a faculty member at the 2006 Tony Hillerman Mystery Writers Conference in Albuquerque, where he presented on the topic of American Indians of the Southwest. His wife, Beverly, is an assistant professor of English at York College. They have two married children, Noah and Summer, and two grandchildren, Ethan and Adrianna. Tim and Bev sponsored study trips for college students on the Lewis and Clark Trail in 2003 and 2005 and to the American Southwest in 2008.